The
Expressive
Actor

The Expressive Actor

INTEGRATED VOICE, MOVEMENT, AND ACTING TRAINING

MICHAEL LUGERING

ILLUSTRATIONS BY LOUIS KAVOURAS

HEINEMANN
PORTSMOUTH, NH

Heinemann
A division of Reed Elsevier Inc.
361 Hanover Street
Portsmouth, NH 03801–3912
www.heinemanndrama.com

Offices and agents throughout the world

Library of Congress Cataloging-in-Publication Data
Lugering, Michael.
    The expressive actor : integrated voice, movement, and acting training / Michael Lugering.
        p. cm.
    Includes bibliographical references and index.
    ISBN-13: 978-0-325-00963-6 (pbk. : alk. paper)
    ISBN-10: 0-325-00963-5
    1. Movement (Acting). 2. Voice culture. 3. Acting. I. Title.
PN2071.M6L84 2007
792.028—dc22   2006033946

Editor: Cheryl Kimball
Production: Lynne Costa
Cover design: Jenny Jensen Greenleaf
Cover and interior illustrations: Louis Kavouras
Typesetter: Valerie Levy / Drawing Board Studios
Manufacturing: Louise Richardson

Printed in the United States of America on acid-free paper
11 10 09 08 07   VP   1 2 3 4 5

Contents

Prologue
Goals, Context, and Perspective

This book has several goals:

1. To present an integrated method of voice, movement, and acting training
2. To emphasize the important role the body plays in the expression of feeling
3. To develop a practical technical vocabulary that objectively describes the physical life of thought and feeling in the voice and the body
4. To present a repeatable method of daily preparation that can be practiced without the assistance of others to keep the actor's voice and body supple, expressive, and ready for the rigorous demands of rehearsal and performance

With few exceptions, acting, voice, and movement training are currently treated as separate disciplines, taught by separate teachers, written about in separate books, and addressed separately in rehearsal and performance. Typically, the diligent acting student travels from voice class to movement class to acting class, often with no formal instruction in how these seemingly isolated disciplines work together. But a detailed examination of individual parts does not always render a clear view of the working whole. Imagine learning to ride a bicycle one part at a time—practicing peddling one day, balance the next, followed by a day of steering. Just as the line of a mountain range can only be understood by moving away from it and standing too close to a painting can distort its full effect (Best 1974), an isolated study of voice, movement, and acting often fails to render a comprehensive understanding of the whole.

An integrated method of acting, voice, and movement training requires a thoughtful reexamination of the manner in which we think about the acting process and ourselves. Western thinking has traditionally asserted that the body is something other than the self. The mind is viewed as boundless, creative, eternal, and often brilliant; it is the seat and center of the self. The body, on the other hand, is viewed as limited, temporal, dull—and sometimes dirty, bad, or even stupid. Thinking of our body as simply an object, a vessel, a physical container that holds or houses a person, devalues the importance of our body and encourages us to disassociate ourselves from our physical experience. The psychologist James I. Kepner (1993) asserts that "when we make our body . . . an 'it' instead of an 'I' we make ourselves less than we are."

Without question, actor training has been influenced by this biased view of the body. As a result, contemporary actors tend to think their way into the characters they play and often ignore and neglect their bodies. They analyze the script, concentrate, remember, daydream, and fantasize—all mental activities—in a quest for vivid and authentic human feeling. They use their intellect to create subtext, inner monologues, and character biographies. Above all, they attempt to *believe* in everything their characters do and say. It is important to recognize that *believing* something to be true is virtually synonymous with *thinking* something to be true. As Phillip B. Zarelli (1995) rightly points out, "believing is devoid of any reference to the body; there is no assertion that believing needs to be embodied." The contemporary actor often creates emotion and character through an act of sheer mental determination and willpower.

There are numerous benefits to these and other mental methods of preparation. However, an overemphasis on the intellect has led a generation of actors to neglect the important role that the voice and body play in the expression of thought and feeling. All too often vocal and physical training is given second-class status. Mental methods of preparation are viewed as all-important, organic, authentic, and honest, while physical methods of preparation are viewed as supplemental, peripheral, inorganic, and even nonemotional. Our appreciation of voice and body training is often limited to technical niceties such as the importance of standing up straight, breathing properly, resonating well, and speaking clearly. Many wrongly assume that voice and body training is to the actor what learning to type might be to the writer. The physical properties of the voice and body, though important, are rarely viewed as rich psychological resources.

Integrated methods of voice, movement, and acting training cannot thrive in such a discriminatory environment. The mind and the body need to be accepted as equal partners in the creative process, and for that to happen we need to acknowledge that feeling is not merely an isolated mental event but also a rich physical experience. Stanislavski (Moore 1960), the famous Russian master acting teacher, said, "The first fact is that the elements of the human soul and the particles of the human body are indivisible." Richard Schechner (1973, 132), an innovative contemporary theatre practitioner, goes so far as to state it this way:

> All performance work begins and ends with the body. When I talk of spirit or mind or feelings or psyche, I mean dimensions of the body. The body is an organism of endless adaptability. A knee can think, a finger can laugh, a belly cry, a brain walk, a buttock listen. All the body's sensory, intellectual and emotional functions can be performed by many organs. Changes in mood are reflected in changes in chemistry, blood pressure, breathing, pulse, vascular dilation, sweating, and so on; and many so-called involuntary activities can be trained and consciously controlled.

When the actor learns to move correctly, the internal and the external, the psychological and physical, the mind and the body, are engaged simultaneously. When a sophisticated level of integration is achieved, physical flexibility and dexterity are linked directly to emotional flexibility and dexterity. When the body learns efficient and coordinated ways of *moving* and *sounding*, it simultaneously learns efficient and coordinated ways of *thinking* and *feeling*. The best actors have varied and flexible bodies capable of a myriad of physical adjustments that never stifle or inhibit feeling but rather serve to inform feeling, shape it, and direct it. It is possible to reach a level of flexibility and expressiveness of such quality that every physical action is simultaneously an emotional one. In time, the body comes to be viewed as a rich psychological playground—a malleable physical medium through which thought and feeling are experienced and organized.

The body is the means by which concrete physical experience is directly felt and immediately sensed; it exists in the real, material world, not as a mental concept, idea, or notion. Consequently, the language of the body is specific, concrete, objective, and above all practical. This allows us to develop a technical vocabulary that accurately describes our physical experience. One of the reasons actor training has lagged behind dance and music training is that it has failed to develop a codified technical vocabulary that describes the physical properties of the actor's craft. Actors are in desperate need of a series of technical terms that describe the physical process of acting. These specialized terms would be as useful to the actor as *tempo* and *meter, plié* and *leap,* are to the musician and the dancer.

A technical vocabulary is the foundation for technical exercises. A practical and reliable working vocabulary makes it possible to create a series of flexible and repeatable exercises designed to strengthen, develop, and maintain the actor's instrument. The most effective of these are solo exercises (like the the musician's musical scales and the dancer's ballet barre) that allow the actor to practice daily without the assistance of others. Whether we like it or not, the most reliable practice method for all artists is a solitary activity in which they diligently, committedly, and painstakingly perfect their craft in isolation. Unfortunately, many acting exercises require a partner, a script, and sometimes even a director or a teacher. This more than any other factor has limited the actor's technique. When developing the actor's instrument depends on outside assistance, the actor practices less frequently. The result is limited growth and arrested development. If acting technique is ever to garner the respect of music and dance training, it will be as a method of solitary daily practice.

Finally, actor training that meets the demands of the new century requires a postmodern understanding of technique. The actor's physical, vocal, and psychological training must be integrated. Progressive methods of actor training place voice/body and thought/feeling on equal footing, with no aspect of the human person given pride of place. The next wave of actor training requires a unified method of training the *total actor* that is too comprehensive to be labeled as either psychological or physical, internal or external, in which the content of acting, voice, and movement classes mixes, mingles, overlaps, and ideally becomes indistinguishable. The actor will not study the parts— voice, movement, acting—but a single integrated discipline—*expression itself.* In the not-too-distant future, acting teachers, voice teachers, movement teachers, and their students will work as a team, sharing a common vocabulary, a similar method of training, and a common set of exercises. I mean this book as a step in this right direction.

Acknowledgments

When I first began developing this work, I had no intentions of writing a book and now find myself somewhat remiss in remembering all the various resources and references that shaped my thinking and influenced my exploration. Consequently, the business of acknowledging my indebtedness to others is somewhat difficult.

I am indebted to many great philosophers, scholars, scientists, teachers, students, actors, and other theatre artists. I have included a substantial bibliography at the end of the book for anyone interested in retracing at least part of my journey. In places in the text, I mention the names of authors and/or the title of books that have contributed to my thinking. However, I fear my obligation to others who are not referenced directly is often greater than might be gathered from the few references in the text.

In an attempt to create a working manual for the actor rather than an academic document, I have regretfully forgone footnotes all together. They proved too cumbersome and academic for the actor in the studio.

With respect to indebtedness, I am most respectful of the enduring legacy of Stanislavski, in particular his *Method of Physical Action*, which shaped and influenced my discussion of *expressive action* presented here. I am equally indebted to Jerzy Grotowski, Michael Chekhov, Richard Schechner, to the aesthetic philosophy of F. S. C. Northrop, Susanne K. Langer, John Dewey, David Best as well as the psychological writings of Edward W. L. Smith, James I. Kepner, and Stanley Keleman.

With respect to practical experience, my initial voice and body training with master teacher Kristin Linklater was invaluable and profound. Her influence and wisdom will be readily evident to students familiar with her work. Additionally, the time I spent at the Alexander Training Institute in Santa Monica, California remains a great resource. Invariably, I am reminded by others of the similarities between the physical method of training presented here and the movement vocabulary of Rudolf Laban. Though my practical and academic links to his work are minimal, I am flattered to be held in such great company.

Most importantly, I must acknowledge the work of Erick Hawkins and the *Erick Hawkins Dance Company*. The voice and body exercises presented in this book are adaptations of many of the physical exercises, which comprise the *Erick Hawkins Dance Technique*. Erick Hawkins was a master dancer, choreographer, and teacher. After a serious injury to his knee, he began to question the strenuous muscular approach to movement present in classical ballet and the popular modern dance technique espoused by his first wife Martha Graham. Working in his studio with his newly formed company, he began to develop a natural approach to movement that worked in harmony with the biomechanics of the human body. The *Erick Hawkins Dance Technique* is characterized by free-flowing movement patterns, economy, ease, and efficiency. Though I never met the late Erick Hawkins, I am deeply indebted to the *Erick Hawkins Dance Company* for their patience and graciousness during the time I studied with them in New York City; in particular, I wish to thank Louis Kavouras, company member and principle dancer, without whose guidance and direction this book would not have been possible.

The improvisational studies presented in this book have their roots in the choreography classes of Lucia Dlugoszewski, the late wife of Erick Hawkins, who served as artistic director, choreographer, and composer during the time that I studied extensively with the company.

I must also thank the Board of Directors at the *Expressive Actor*, a 501 3(c), nonprofit organization (www.expressiveactor.org) that offers national and international workshops and training intensives, which promotes the sharing of this integrated method of actor training with others.

Additionally, I must thank my colleagues at the University of Nevada, Las Vegas and the many fine students there who shared in the creation of this work. Finally, my editors: Lisa Barnett, Cheryl Kimball, Leigh Peake, Lynne Costa, and everyone who contributed to publication of this book at Heinemann have my deepest thanks.

Introduction
Expression and the Actor

E *xpression* is the process of revealing in movement, sound, and
words what one thinks and feels. There is an important distinction between *having* or *experiencing* a thought or feeling and
expressing that thought or feeling. Everyone experiences thoughts and
feelings that are deeply moving and to which he or she is fully committed. However, not everyone is able to reveal in movements, sounds,
and words the rich content of his or her mental and emotional life.
There is nothing more frustrating than having a thought or feeling and
not being able to find an appropriate and effective way to express it.

Most of us would like to express ourselves better, and we genu-
inely admire individuals who seem to have mastered the art of doing
so. Any act of expression—whether in a coffee shop, a classroom, a
subway, a synagogue, a courtroom, or the back seat of a car—when
executed skillfully can be said to be artful. Sometimes inspiration
descends, and thoughts and feelings miraculously find their perfect
and complete expression. At other times, we are not so lucky. Often
we find ourselves mumbling and fumbling for an appropriate way to
express ourselves. In moments of great passion, we are often at a total loss. Rarely does the caliber of our daily discourse possess the grace,
skill, power, sensitivity, and ease characteristic of artful expression. As
Aristotle said, "Anyone can become angry—that is easy. But to be angry
with the right person, to the right degree, at the right time, for the right
purpose, in the right way—that is not easy."

This is exactly what the actor is required to do: express the right
feeling, with the right person, to the right degree, at the right time, for
the right purpose, and in the right way. Actors are society's best mod-
els for the expression of life's most complex thoughts and feelings.
Most characters in dramatic literature express themselves better than
the average person. Playwrights do more than merely reveal human
experience; they explain it, question it, challenge it, and sometimes
change it, often by empowering a character, even if for a single moment, with an almost supernatural gift of self-expression. This perfect
organization of thinking, feeling, moving, sounding, and speaking is
human expression at its best.

This is not to suggest that there are not examples of disorganized and incoherent expression in some of the theatre's greatest plays. Actors are often called upon to move, speak, feel, and think in less than ideal ways. Surprisingly, creating characters that express themselves in inefficient, unnatural, and clumsy ways can be more difficult than creating characters that express themselves very well. In the theater, even inefficient, unnatural, and clumsy expression must be artful. A prerequisite for expressing a thought and feeling poorly on the stage is knowing how to express that thought and feeling masterfully.

The best acting often looks so spontaneous and effortless that it is easy to assume that no training or technical skill is required. Appearances are deceiving. Great actors, like great athletes, make the most sophisticated activities look easy because they have highly developed technical skills. This type of expertise strikes at the heart of what it means to be a skilled actor. It is the great dividing line that separates the professional from the amateur. To some degree, all actors bring to rehearsal and performance a somewhat limited and habitual method of expressing themselves. Conscientious actors recognize that there are certain types of emotional, mental, physical, and verbal expression readily at their disposal, while other types of expression remain elusive and inaccessible. Even actors who can express their personal thoughts and feelings with relative ease and grace often have trouble expressing the complex thoughts and feelings of the characters they portray. Without training and technique, even the most talented actors eventually find themselves holding the short end of the stick.

The central premise of this book, then, is that the study of acting should begin with human expression, rather than with scripts, character, language, style, or performance. The study of expression provides the essential human perspective that is the springboard for exploring the entire acting process. Under the label of expression, all the seemingly disparate elements of the actor's craft—voice, breath, body, feeling, and language—are synthesized into a single course of study.

Deeply rooted in process, the method presented here is concerned not so much with *why* we express ourselves but *how*. Greed, enthusiasm, pride, disgust, resentment, frustration, or joy can be expressed in many ways. Yet the process with which these different thoughts and feelings are organized into meaningful forms of vocal and bodily expression is consistent and similar. Consequently, a special type of physical training can be developed that prepares the body to express thought and feeling. And when we become aware of the physical process with which we express a *single* thought and feeling, we simultaneously become aware of the physical process with which we express *every* thought and feeling. The technique begins with a series of universal principles of expression focusing on the shared pattern or structure by which all thoughts and feelings find a physical life in the voice and body. These principles encompass specific directives for the simultaneous development of the actor's physical, vocal, and emotional instrument. They transcend any specific acting style, focusing on universal aspects of human communication present in all drama, from Shakespeare to Simon, Wycherly to Wasserstein, and Molière to Mamet.

The method presented here is *preparatory*. It does not address the important collaboration that occurs between actors and directors in connection with a script. Ideally, the integrated physical, vocal, and emotional training presented here will be augmented by practical work with the script in the classroom and the rehearsal hall and during performance. Also, detailed speech and language training, interpretation and analysis, character study, and style, while important subjects, receive only cursory treatment in these chapters. I hope to extend the ideas, concepts, and principles presented here in a second book.

About the Book

The book is organized as follows:

> *Prologue:* a preliminary discussion of expression, technique, actor training, and art.
>
> *Part I, Principles of Expressive Action:* a theoretical discussion of the universal process with which all human beings organize thought and feeling into physical forms of expression.
>
> *Part II, Principles of Voice and Body:* a practical discussion of the manner in which the body, breath, and voice function in the context of human expression.
>
> *Part III, Voice and Body Exercises:* a series of integrated voice and body exercises designed to develop the freedom, flexibility, dexterity, coordination, range, and power needed for dynamic and effective expression.
>
> *Part IV, Improvisation:* a series of flexible improvisational studies designed to cultivate a healthy respect for impulse, spontaneity, creativity, language, and character while simultaneously

expanding and broadening your imagination and increasing expressive potential.

Epilogue: an aesthetic primer intended to question, challenge, and stimulate discussion about the nature of artful expression in the context of acting and theatre.

The separation of theory from practice is deliberate. The principles of expression and the principles of voice and body are in the front of the book; the voice and body exercises and the improvisational studies are in the back. There is a time and place to think about technique and a time to experience it in the body. The best instruction provides a daily dose of both. When I teach, I weave theory and practice together in an almost improvisatory way. It is difficult to replicate that type of synergy in a written text. As a point of departure, I suggest you first read and explore the theory in several sittings. When the principles are fully understood, you can then explore the voice and body exercises and the improvisational studies simultaneously and sequentially, at your own pace, returning frequently to the theory for guidance and direction.

With time and repetition, both the mind and body are educated. What at first seems confusing is ultimately clarified in the act of doing. It will take two or three years to master the skills presented here, and even then the exercises must be practiced regularly so that your instrument remains strong, free, supple, and expressive. Diligence and patience pave the best road to success.

Expressive Action

Expressive actions are the fundamental building blocks of the actor's art and craft. The term *action* has its deepest roots in the term *drama,* which comes from the Greek word *dran* meaning *to do.* Characters in plays tell their stories by doing things—promising their love, waging war, stealing money, confessing mistakes, and betraying friends, among a host of other human behaviors skillfully penned by imaginative playwrights. This *doing* that lies at the very heart of drama is commonly referred to as *action.* Because actors, directors, theater critics, and scholars use the term *action* so frequently and often somewhat differently, it is important to clarify the exact meaning of the term *expressive action* used here.

An expressive action is any physical action that simultaneously contains and reveals thought and feeling. Through expressive action, the physical life of a thought or feeling is revealed through the voice and body. Expressive actions are the smallest units of human communication. They can be as small as a shrug of the shoulders, a disapproving look, or a simple handshake. Scolding a child, confessing a mistake, standing your ground, turning your back on a friend, lying through your teeth, and screaming bloody murder are also good examples of expressive actions. An expressive action, though rooted in movement and activity, is not merely a physical task. Strictly speaking, closing a car door, flipping on a light switch, folding a newspaper, and drinking a glass of wine are physical tasks, not expressive actions. But clear-cut distinctions between an expressive action and a physical task work better in theory than in practice. It is possible to close a car door in a huff, flip on a light switch with trepidation, fold a newspaper sternly, and drink a glass of wine in celebration. In instances like this, these physical tasks can simultaneously be labeled expressive actions.

Most importantly, an expressive action reflects a complex integration of the whole person. In practical terms, this integration can be thought of as the skillful coordination of emotional, physical, and mental experience. The *feeling* provides the necessary drive excitation and energy. The *body* is the facilitator responsible for directing and coordinating the physical action and the *mind* is responsible for organizing and cataloging the action into meaningful and differentiated experience. The most important benefit of playing an expressive action is the authentic emotional experience that the physical action creates in the body and voice. Expressive actions simultaneously get the actor moving and feeling. When an expressive action is played successfully, the physical action itself has intrinsic emotional properties. Suppose I ask you to throw a chair against the wall several times. If you are supple and receptive to the emotional component of the movement, this physical action might make you angry or frustrated or perhaps giddy and playfully destructive. It is through movement that feeling is created in the body of the actor. When we express ourselves, thought, feeling, and physical action are engaged simultaneously and are seemingly inseparable. As Stanislavski states in *Creating A Role* (1961): "In every *physical action*, unless it is purely mechanical, there is concealed some *inner action*, some feelings."

Sensation + Impulse + Energy + Form = Expressive Action

Expressive action begins with *sensation*. It is important to make a distinction between *passing sensations* and the more complete process of *acting on our sensations*. Passing sensations are those sensory stimuli that fade in and out of our awareness without motivating us to action. For example, as I type, the sound of the furnace, a glimpse of a car moving past the window, and the growling of my stomach move freely in and out of my consciousness, but these passing sensations have not prompted or motivated me to action.

However, if I wave to the neighbor in the passing car, I will have acted on just one of the many sensations filtering through my consciousness. We act on our sensations when we respond to an inner *impulse*. Legendary theater practitioner Jerzy Grotowski defined an impulse as an *in push*—an internal nudge or prompt—that results in an *out push*—an outward physical action that makes expressive action possible (Richards 1995). On a physical level, an impulse manifests itself in waves of energy that are transmitted via nerve endings, muscles, and tissues, through the body.

This surge of energy results in increased respiration, heart rate, adrenaline, and physical activity—the necessary fuel and power that make expressive action possible. Big thoughts and feelings generate high levels of energy in the body; smaller thoughts and feelings generate lower levels of energy.

An expressive action occurs when the increased energy associated with our thoughts and feelings is successfully organized into a *form* that communicates our thoughts and feelings to others. We give form to our thoughts and feelings through the things we *do* and the things we *say*. Essentially, a complex expressive action reflects a synthesis of both verbal and nonverbal forms of communication. Verbal forms of expression encompass everything that can be communicated through language. Movement, gesture, facial expression, body language, and the sound of the voice are nonverbal forms of expression. Ultimately, an expressive action is only complete when our thoughts and feelings find expressive verbal and nonverbal forms in the voice and body.

Describing Expressive Actions

Finding the right words to describe an expressive action is tricky. Unfortunately, the most vital and exciting expressive actions often defy precise verbal description. As David Best (1974) states:

> the expressive meaning of an action, though a characteristic of the movement itself, cannot be explained purely in anatomical, physiological or other scientific terms.

The most popular method of describing an expressive action is to use an active verb: *to confess, to bluff, to tempt,* or *to tease*. A verb is preferred because it provides the actor with something specific to do and roots the action in intention. While this is without question a useful way of describing an expressive action, it is certainly not the only way. For example, to say that a character is *huffing and puffing, spinning like a top,* or *tongue-wagging* is as descriptive as saying that a character wants *to defend* or *to protest.* I have heard actors describe expressive actions with all manner of language, some of which borders on poetry: *as if for the last time, without hesitation,* or *never again.* Any of these simple phrases, among countless others, can suggest, prompt, and lead sensitive actors to playable expressive actions.

Sometimes the best clues for what to call the expressive action are in the script. When Romeo describes Juliet at the masquerade ball, he states: "She does teach the torches to burn bright." Juliet is beaming and radiant. There is nothing wrong with calling her expressive action *torches burning bright.* Sometimes the best labels for an expressive action are nonsensical—*to yuck 'n fluster, to tick and tack, to wee, to gobbledygook.* Sometimes idiomatic expressions are helpful—*to wear your heart on your sleeve, to have a bee in your bonnet,* or *to burst at the seams.* Additionally, it is just as useful to describe an expressive action in physical terms such as *light, direct,* and *fast.* Sometimes expressive actions are referenced to blocking—*when I pick up the book* or *as I come down the stairs.* In the end, it does not matter what we call the expressive action. An expressive action is an expressive action, quite simply, if it is expressive. The appropriateness of an expressive action should not be judged by the words used to describe it but rather the authentic expression of thought and feeling that it creates in the voice and body.

Expressive Actions and Objectives

It is important to distinguish an *expressive action* from an *objective.* An objective—an acting term first articulated by the Russian acting teacher Stanislavski (1936)—is a simple statement of the wants, needs, goals, and desires of a character in a play. Statements such as, "I want to make up for past mistakes," "I wish to better my position," or "I need to save myself from further humiliation," describe the reason or motivation for a character's behavior and are good examples of an objective. Objectives describe *why* a character behaves in a certain way. Expressive actions, on the other hand, such as *to question, to scoff, to berate,* and *to assess,* describe *what* the character is literally doing at a specific moment in the script. An expressive action is a statement of process, describing the means and methods with which the wants, needs, goals, desires, and motivations of the character are fulfilled.

Most often, many expressive actions unite to help the character achieve a single objective. Consider a young boy who wants his mother to let him play outside. Obviously, the young boy's objective is *to go outside and play.* Achieving this goal will require many expressive actions. Consider the following possibilities:

- *To beg* ("Please, please, Mom, can I go outside, please, please?")
- *To abuse* ("You are so mean. I hate you. You never let me do anything.")
- *To negotiate* ("If you let me go outside, I promise I'll clean up my room and do my homework and always say please and thank you.")

If the young boy is successful, all of these smaller individual expressive actions will unite in helping him persuade his mother to let him go outside.

Expressive Actions in Rehearsal

In rehearsal, it is often useful to name the specific expressive action being played. Labeling the action provides a point of reference and assists in structuring and creating a coherent journey for the character. This is not to suggest that every expressive action must be named, discussed, and analyzed. There are so many expressive actions in a single scene of a play that labeling them is all but impossible. Actors tend to label the important actions, the actions they are struggling with, and the ones they discuss with other actors and the director.

Each expressive action that a character plays is like a single bead in a beautiful necklace. Just as many beads unite to create a necklace, many expressive actions unite to create the life of a character in a play. The job of the actor is ultimately to find a specific expressive action to play during each moment of performance. Just as a dancer learns the choreography step by step, or a pianist learns the piece of music finger sequence by finger sequence, the actor also creates an authentic performance one expressive action at a time. The rehearsal process is largely the business of discovering expressive actions that work, testing them, changing them, and ultimately structuring them into a repeatable pattern. The script is a blueprint or road map to expressive action (Harrop 1992). If the actor reads the blueprint well, the expressive actions played will simultaneously reveal thought and feeling, forward the plot, and define the character. In rehearsal, expressive actions sometimes spring forth spontaneously with little or no conscious effort or choice; one is stacked upon another intuitively and instinctively. Others require technique, training, experimentation, experience, and the guidance of a gifted director.

When working with expressive actions, the actor does not create the emotional life of the character by pursuing feeling directly but through outward physical action and activity. Any actor who has sat down with a script and attempted to make emotional notations in the margins—*sad, shocked, confused, angry*—can readily attest to the method's shortcomings. Once having determined the desired feeling, the misguided actor manipulates the voice and body in any manner possible in an attempt to manufacture the authentic emotion. This leads to a mechanical indication or manipulation of feeling, often devoid of sincere feeling. The problem with this direct approach is that feelings cannot be conjured up at will and displayed on demand. Authentic feeling is best induced indirectly through the playing of an expressive action—desperation through acts of pleading and begging; love through acts of praising and cherishing; loss through acts of mourning and reflection. Ultimately, the art of acting lies not in the conscious re-creation of a predetermined emotional state but in finding appropriate expressive actions that indirectly reveal emotion.

The trap of playing a feeling often occurs in big emotional scenes, even for experienced actors where the stakes are usually very high. Consider a scene in which a mother mourns the loss of her child. The emotional demands are clear: the actor must demonstrate a passionate display of grief, loss, and desperation. But it is important not to become sidetracked and start to work for the emotional result. The actor should not begin by trying to conjure up a big sad feeling. Nor is it necessary to feel the emotion completely and fully at the first rehearsal. The desired feeling can only be created with time and exploration. The job of the actor is to create not one big feeling but many small and varied expressive actions that unite to form the larger display of grief. As the actor begins to find specific expressive actions to play in each moment of the scene, the feeling emerges indirectly and spontaneously. Many small expressive actions—*holding your heart, pulling your hair, questioning the facts, cursing the gods, wiping away your tears, maintaining self-control,* and *finding someone to blame*—unite to achieve the total affect of loss and devastation. The more specific and varied the expressive actions found, the clearer and more profound the feeling expressed. With each rehearsal, more specific and detailed expressive actions emerge. The actor works, consciously and unconsciously, to structure the expressive actions into a well-ordered whole. When the actor has found a detailed and specific expressive action for each moment in the scene, the larger display of grief becomes decidedly simpler. In the end, the result is a powerful display of feeling that is well structured, repeatable, and above all authentic.

Exploring on Your Own

Select an expressive action from the list below:

to beg	to warn	to apologize
to promise	to scold	to praise

Compose a simple but flexible piece of text for the selected expressive action. (For example, for *to promise* you might compose: "I will never tell another lie.") Play your expressive action several times while delivering the piece of text you have composed. Rest. Repeat using other expressive actions listed above or with other expressive actions of your own choosing.

First and Second Functions

The philosopher F. S. C. Northrop (1962) asserts that we have two distinct ways of knowing and understanding our world—a *sensing way* and a *thinking way*—and that virtually anything can be known or understood from these two distinct perspectives. For example, today it is 102 degrees where I live. If I leave my air-conditioned home and walk outside to pick up the newspaper, I know or understand that it is hot outside. My immediate sensory experience informs me that today is a scorcher. I feel the heat on my skin and through my clothes. To understand something in a sensing way is to know it directly and experientially. On the other hand, if I sit in my air-conditioned home, look out my window, and read the thermometer hanging on the wall outside, I can also know or understand that it is very hot outside. In this instance, I know that it is hot in a thinking way. I know it indirectly, from reasoning and using my intellect. I do not feel the heat directly but rather infer or deduce that when the thermometer passes the century mark it is extremely hot outside. Northrop identified the information that we receive from our senses as a *first functional way of knowing*, and the information that we receive through thinking as a *second functional way of knowing*.

A deeper understanding of expressive action is aided by making a similar distinction between the two distinct ways that we can know or understand an expressive action: a *sensing way* and a *thinking way*, or an *expressive action in its first function* and an *expressive action in its second function*.

The Foreign Traveler and the Departing Bus

You are walking down the street and notice a foreign traveler frantically waving his arms and calling out in a desperate attempt to stop a departing bus. You sense that something unfortunate has just happened, but you are not sure what, because the traveler is calling out in a language you do not understand. Despite your confusion, you immediately perceive and catalogue a myriad of physical and vocal sensations into a recognizable expression of feeling. The foreign traveler's feelings, though hard to describe in words, reflect alarm, panic, fear, and desperation.

Because you do not understand the language of the foreign traveler, you have very little intellectual information to help you determine exactly what has happened. Your information is limited to what you have been able to sense directly by the sound of the foreign traveler's voice and the movement of his body. If someone standing on the street corner were to ask you what just happened, you would probably respond, "I don't know." This is only half true. Although you don't know specifically what happened, you have very accurate intuitive information about the emotional state of the foreign traveler. He is without question alarmed, panicked, and desperate. Without recourse to thinking, you were able to assimilate his vocal and physical activity into a meaningful understanding of his emotional state. You have a very clear understanding of the foreign traveler's expressive action in its first function.

You, like most human beings, are a curious creature, and your intellect desires to make logical sense of your recent sensory experience. You speculate that the foreign traveler must have gotten off at the wrong bus stop by accident and was attempting to reboard the departing bus. Coincidentally, you discover that a friend also witnessed the same event. You ask your friend what just happened. Your friend, like you, is not sure, but speculates the foreign traveler must have left something important on the bus. You and your friend's differing intellectual interpretations of your sensory experience illustrate a sincere attempt to understand the foreign traveler's expressive action in its second function. Unfortunately, without language—the most effective method of expressing thought—understanding the foreign traveler's expressive action in its second function is decidedly more difficult. Neither you nor your friend knows exactly why the foreign traveler was chasing the departing bus.

But suppose you *are* fluent in the language of the foreign traveler. As you turn the corner, you hear him calling out, "Wait! Wait! That's the last bus to the airport this evening!" Now you have a complete and accurate understanding of the foreign traveler's expressive action in its second function. He was not, as you and your friend had speculated, trying to reboard the departing bus but attempting to board it for the first time. This intellectual understanding requires two sets of cognitive skills. First, you must understand the meaning of the words being spoken—"Wait! Wait! That's the last bus to the airport this evening!" Second, you must have the mental wherewithal to determine that missing the last bus to the airport is a less-than-promising situation, especially when traveling in a foreign country.

Intellect and Intuition

A deeper understanding of an expressive action in its first and second functions is aided by examining the two parts of the human brain that process sensing and thinking information—the intuition and the intellect. My understanding of the differences between the *intuition* and *intellect* are influenced by the philosophical writings of Susanne K. Langer (1942) and the psychologist Daniel Goleman (1995).

Intellect
The intellect is located in the space between our ears. It is what we commonly refer to as our *mind*. It is the rational, logical information center responsible for processing thought. Reasoning, identifying, defining, classifying, analyzing, comparing, and interpreting are all mental activities made possible by the extraordinary power of the intellect. Our intellect enables us to follow directions, balance our checkbook, carry on conversations, read books, and send spaceships to the moon. This superior intelligence distinguishes human beings from all other creatures. Surprisingly, while human beings have a great capacity for intellectual knowledge, at birth the intellect is virtually undeveloped. Our intellectual understanding of the world is acquired almost exclusively through life experience.

When speaking on an expressive action in its second function, we are referencing the thinking component of the expressive action, made possible by the power of the intellect. With respect to expression, the intellect makes verbal communication possible. Language is essentially an intellectual activity. Words are the building blocks for thought, or perhaps better stated, the wrapper in which thoughts are delivered. Through language, we give form to our intellectual life. In the course of a single day's activities, we give verbal form to an almost inconceivable amount of cognitive information: "Wait! Wait! That's the last bus to the airport this evening!" "The square of the hypotenuse of a right triangle is equal to the sum of the squares of the two adjacent sides." It is not a coincidence that human beings—the most intellectually evolved living creatures—are the only species with a highly codified system of verbal and written symbols that unite to form a complex language. Without an advanced intellect, language is all but impossible. Fortunately, this unique intellectual ability enables us to understand and describe the richness of our emotional and mental lives.

The link between thinking and speaking is so great that often they are assumed to be a singular activity. We are said to *speak our minds* and *voice our opinions*. Furthermore, to state that someone is *articulate* is an acknowledgment of intelligence. People who speak well are automatically assumed to be smart. Often, the relationship between thinking and speaking is extended to listening and learning. To have *heard something* is synonymous with *knowing something*. Perhaps this is why it is said that a wise man is a good listener.

Anyone who has acquired a second language is painfully aware that language is an intellectual activity. Many bilingual speakers, even after years of exposure to a second language, are hindered in their expression because much of their thinking process remains in their native language.

Intuition

The intuition, by contrast, is the sensing, feeling information system associated with the body. It is responsible for processing all the data received from the senses. *Sense* in this context is not limited to sight, sound, smell, taste, and touch but includes all that can be described as *felt experience*. Our most basic human desires—to seek pleasure and avoid pain, for food, companionship, and sex—are all a product of our intuition. Our intuition informs us when we are tired, whether we are hot or cold, have a headache, or are sick to our stomach. Our perceptions of color and texture are made possible by the intuition. Our intuition instructs us that flowers are beautiful and that dark alleys are to be avoided at night. It is how we know that it is evening without looking at a clock, that it is going to rain when we have not heard a weather report, that the dog we have never seen before is dangerous, or that the ladder we are standing on is wobbly and unsafe. The intuition provides us with a type of sensory knowledge that is infinite, largely immeasurable, and often goes unnoticed in the course of daily living. It is a type of *physical intelligence* or *body knowledge* that is innate and instinctive. Our intuitive understanding of the world is, more or less, prewired at birth and appears to be given to everyone in seemingly equal degrees.

When speaking of an expressive action in its first function, we are referring to its feeling/sensing component made possible by the power of the intuition. All nonverbal forms of expression—movement, gesture, body language, facial expression, eye contact, touch, the sound of the voice—are governed largely by the intuition. Most importantly, the intuition makes emotional expression possible. Through the body and the movement of the body we experience, express, and give form to our feelings. The famous neuroscientist Antonio Damasio (1999) asserts that while feeling is impossible without some sort of cerebral action, the *body*, not the *brain*, is the main stage for our feelings. We often think, wrongly, of feeling as something going on inside us—a subconscious interior event that is internal and seemingly hidden from view, and somehow separate from our bodily movements. In doing so, we devalue the rich physical component of our feelings. The feelings we so commonly think of as residing in our heads are traveling through our bodies on caravans of hormones and enzymes, busily organizing our muscles, bones, blood, and breath—our whole bodies—into complex patterns that allow us to experience and express our feelings. As David Best (1974) states, feeling is not simply some added ingredient mixed with or placed on top of our bodily movements but rather a by-product of movement itself. There are not two separate things—a movement and a feeling—but one thing—a movement that possesses or contains feeling. Idiomatic expressions like *sorehead, lily-livered, no backbone, hair-raising, choked up, bleeding heart, tight-ass, nose out of joint,* and *blood-boiling* are a testament to the physical nature of our feelings. In fact, the Latin origin of the word *emotion* is *e + movere*, meaning *to move out* or *away from*. It seems that without motion, *e-motion* is impossible.

It is sometimes difficult to grasp that we feel without the assistance of our intellect. We do not determine what we are feeling in the same manner that we look at our watch and *think* we are late for dinner or read a road map and *think* we have made a wrong turn. Rather, we simply *sense* that we are sad, happy, or angry. It is not necessary to *think* that the sad individual has lost a good friend, that the happy individual has won the lottery, or that the angry individual has been passed over for a promotion. We become aware of our own feelings and the feelings of others in much the same way that we sense watermelon is sweet, that our feet are wet, or that flowers smell pretty. It is a nonintellectual, intuitive process.

Even more surprising is the concept that feeling, because it is a physical experience, takes on a recognizable physical form. As a part of our genetic heritage, the human brain is equipped with a built-in structuring device that enables us to organize gestures, facial expressions, postures, stances, and a host of vocal sounds into meaningful forms of emotional expression, in much the same way our intellect allows us to process language into meaningful forms of verbal expression. The pelvis, legs, feet, hands, arms, head, face, lips—the whole body—are capable of organizing themselves in an infinite number of meaningful patterns. These unique forms instruct us that the young boy mumbling with his head in his hands is down in the dumps and the young girl giggling with glee, a sparkle in her eye and a grin a mile wide, is walking on top of the world.

In fact, the physical form of a feeling is so imprinted on our consciousness that we often infer feeling in places where actual feelings do not exist. For example, a jagged red line pounding across a computer screen might appear angry or hostile, while a pink, yellow, and baby-blue line dancing across the computer screen in harmonious, explosive jumps might appear joyous and celebratory. The philosopher Susanne K. Langer (1953) states that when she was a young child, the heavy, dark, and intricate chairs in her grandmother's living room appeared to her as stern, frightful, and foreboding. Of course, chairs in the living room and colored lines on a computer screen are inanimate objects incapable of feeling anything. Nonetheless, their physical form in some manner suggests a feeling.

Our perception of the physical form of a feeling is so instinctual and automatic that our conscious mind often fails to recognize these forms even when they are right in front of us. Gilbert Ryle (1949) cites an example of a foreign visitor who is taken on a tour of Cambridge

University: the lecture halls, the dormitories, the classrooms, the laboratories, the library, the administrative offices, the playing field, the chapel—the whole campus. At the end of the tour, he asks: "This is all very good, but where is the university?" What he has failed to recognize is that in examining the classrooms, the library, and the laboratories in front of him, he has in fact *seen* the university. It is just as illogical to examine the piercing eyes, clinched teeth, tight lips, and stifled breath of a person fuming with anger and say, "I see all of this, but where is the anger?" Feeling and bodily movement are inseparable. Asking how the feeling got into the body is not unlike asking how the fruit got into the apple, the wind into the hurricane, or the fire into the sun. When the body moves, we experience our feelings, and through movement, we express our feelings.

We should also note that the physical sensations associated with feeling do not simply reference the body but include all the various oral sensations that unite in the process of making sound. Sound is a rich, sensuous physical experience. The various vibrations, tones, pitches, resonances—the buzzes, pops, bangs, moans, murmurs, and hisses that form the sounds we make—are a bodily process and are equally filled with emotional meaning. Sound is best viewed as the oral extension of the body. Through the sound of the voice, the feelings that live and reside in the body speak.

In summary, language allows us to give form to our thoughts, and our body enables us to give form to our feelings. We have both words and bodily movements as a means of expression. Without them, it would be impossible to fully express our thoughts and feelings. Just as language is ill equipped to express feeling, the body is equally ill equipped to express thought. As David Best (1974) asserts, should someone experiencing sadness cry out, "Leave me alone!" or "I don't know what to do!" the words themselves, without the physical presence of the sad person, would provide little information about the emotional state of the individual. The person could just as well be angry, overwhelmed, or embarrassed. The words are not expressing the feeling but rather the thoughts accompanying and associated with the feeling.

It might be argued that emotion can be expressed in words by stating, "I am sad," or "I feel sad." However, this fails to take into account the important distinction between *reporting* or *describing* a feeling and *experiencing* and *expressing* a feeling. Similarly, the body is ill equipped to express thought. Sign language aside, no amount of pointing, gesturing, or signaling can ever take the place of language. Anyone who has ever visited a foreign country without knowing the language can attest to the inability of desperate gestures to communicate even the simplest of information.

The differences between an expressive action in its first and second function are summarized below:

First Function	Second Function
Body	Mind
Doing	Saying
Feeling	Speaking
Intuition	Intellect
Nonverbal	Verbal
Sensing	Thinking
Movement	Language

What About Poetry?

It has been asserted that language is an intellectual activity ill equipped to express emotion. The obvious question that then arises is, "What about poetry? Doesn't it express feeling?" The answer is of course a resounding yes, with one important stipulation. Words are inanimate, intellectual, logical constructions that are, in the strictest sense, incapable of "physically" feeling. Words and language cannot feel in the same visceral and organic way that a living, breathing person does. However, when spoken by a sensitive speaker, they can convey an intense *awareness* of feeling. In this sense, language becomes emotional only when it finds a physical and sensorial life in the body. Poetry is a special type of language that speaks not to the *head* but to the *heart*. It serves to point, lead, guide, evoke, arouse, suggest, and direct the sensitive speaker and intuitive listener toward specific bodily sensations commonly associated with feeling. Perhaps the most effective literary device for evoking feeling is rhythm. Some lines race and soar with a dynamic emotional immediacy, while others move with a slow deliberateness that has a very different emotional effect. Rhyme, alliteration, assonance, diction, structure, imagery, allusions, illusions, symbols, metaphors, and a host of other literary and rhetorical devices are employed, both consciously and unconsciously, to arouse and entice the body to feel. In this respect, words can have a powerful emotional effect.

Exploring on Your Own

Rent a foreign film in a language that you do not understand. Watch the film with the subtitles turned off. Without the assistance of language, you will be experiencing much of the film in the first function. See how much emotional information you can glean by simply observing the body and listening to the sound of the speaker's voice.

Physical Properties

In this chapter, we will look more closely at the physical properties that unite to create an expressive action in its first function (Chapter 2). All expressive actions share a similar set of physical properties that can be readily identified by a skilled observer. Focusing on the physical properties of an expressive action encourages a practical and experiential understanding of the emotional process. Additionally, an understanding of the physical properties provides a useful technical vocabulary for the actor.

Expressive actions are not unlike people in that there are certain *major physical properties* that all human beings share and certain *minor physical properties* specific and particular to each individual. Ideally, human beings have two eyes, two arms, two legs, one heart, a pair of lungs, ten fingers and toes, and so on. In addition to these major physical properties, there are other minor physical properties specific to each individual that make them unique and different. While human beings have two eyes, no two eyes are the same. This is true for a host of other secondary characteristics: weight, height, skin color, eye color, hairline, and so on.

Expressive actions also have major physical properties—things shared in common that make them similar—and minor physical properties—things that make them unique and different. My understanding of the major and minor properties of an expressive action reflect an assimilation and adaptation of the ideas of somatic psychologists James I. Kepner (1993), Edward W. L. Smith (1985), Jack Lee Rosenberg (1985), and the movement analysis method of Rudolph Von Laban (1974).

The Expressive Cycle: Major Physical Properties

The expressive cycle is a blueprint outlining the manner in which all living creatures function and operate in their environment. It articulates the universal structure by which the major physical properties of an expressive action are organized into meaningful emotional expression. The expressive cycle describes the progressive and orderly flow with which an expressive action begins, matures, and subsides. As illustrated in Figure 3.1, each wave of the expressive cycle has a clearly defined beginning, middle, and end representing one complete unit of living, which corresponds to the execution of one complete expressive action.

It is useful to think of the expressive cycle in three stages. The *initiation phase* is characterized by an internal imbalance or agitation, which prompts and prepares the body for action. The *development phase* is the substantive portion, characterized by outward action and physical activity. The *resolution phase* is characterized by feelings of

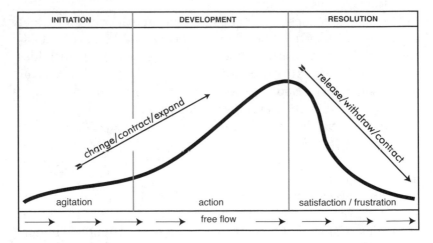

Figure 3.1 Expressive Cycle

satisfaction and gratification or frustration and discomfort, depending on whether the expressive action was successful or unsuccessful.

The sequential journey of the expressive cycle from start to finish, beginning to end, agitation to action to satisfaction, has intrinsic rhythmical properties that are similar to the ocean's waves. Each wave of the ocean has a clearly defined beginning, middle, and end. The wave rises, swells, crests, cascades, and finally subsides. The end of one wave is followed directly by the start of a new wave. Though each individual wave is a separate and unique event, when sequenced one right after another a rhythmical pattern emerges. Similarly, a series of successive waves of the expressive cycle sets up a rhythmical pattern that can be seen in the comings and goings of daily life. Saying good morning, taking a sip of coffee, stretching the arms and shoulders, and opening a newspaper are each individual and separate actions with a clearly defined beginning, middle, and end, yet when connected in a sequence they unite to form a larger rhythmical pattern of someone's morning ritual. Whether the seas of life be choppy or calm, the tides high or low, skillful expression rises, swells, crests, cascades, and falls with rhythmical harmony.

The expressive cycle is created by five interrelated components—energy, orientation, size, progression, and flow—that unite to form the major properties of an expressive action.

Energy: Charge/Release

Energy refers to the relative degree of physical and psychological vitality and power present in the body. A high level of energy is identified as a charge, a low level of energy as a release. Charge and release, working together, making expression possible. When we reach out to shake someone's hand, the building up of energy necessary to extend the arm is identified as a charge. After completing the handshake, the return of the arm back to its resting position is identified as a release. The charge phase of the expressive cycle reflects the conscious, mobile, and active portion of human expression; the release phase reflects a letting go—a semiconscious, passive "nondoing" that returns the body to a state of equilibrium and balance.

Orientation: Contact/Withdraw

Orientation refers to the directional force that motivates the action of the individual in the environment. An individual makes contact with the environment to fulfill specific physical and psychological needs and withdraws when these needs have been satisfied. A state of contact refers to an individual with a strong outward/external orientation. It is characterized by a forward and advancing outward movement. Similarly, a state of withdrawal refers to an individual with a strong inward/internal orientation. It is characterized by a retreating inward movement. In integrated expression, contact and withdrawal work as a team, making expression possible. When we reach out to shake someone's hand, the process of extending the arm results in contact with the environment. After completing the handshake, the return of the arm back to its resting position results in a withdrawal from the environment. Outward observable interaction with the environment characterizes the contact phase of the expressive cycle while the withdrawal phase is characterized by a period of internalization, reflection, assessment, and evaluation.

Size: Expand/Contract

Size refers to the physical range or volume of a movement. Changes in the size of the body are made possible by the bending and unbending of various joints in the body. Movements that involve lengthening and elongating the body are expanded. Movements that involve folding or recoiling the body are contracted. Expansion and contraction work together in expressive action, moving the muscles and bones of the body in an almost infinite number of physical configurations that make expression possible. When we reach out to shake someone's hand, the process of extending the arm requires an expansion of the body. After completing the handshake, the return of the arm back to its resting position requires a contraction of the body.

Progression: Center/Periphery

Progression is the sequence or pathway of a movement through the body. The center of the body is the midsection, specifically the pelvis. The periphery of the body are the parts furthest away from the pelvis—the head, arms, hands, legs, and feet. An expressive action that begins with movement in the center of the body is a centered action. An expressive action that begins with movement on the periphery of the body is a peripheral action. Successful and fluid expressive action often requires that the center of the body and the parts on the periphery work together in an organized manner, creating movement that flows from the middle of the body (the center) outward into the appendages (the periphery). Initiating movement from the pelvis has important ramifications with respect to the expression of feeling. Feelings begin deep in the center of the body and travel outward to the periphery on waves of energy. When we initiate movement from the pelvis, feeling is carried outward from the center of the body to the periphery. This simultaneous outward movement of the physical and psychological is a central component of integrated emotional expression.

Flow: Free/Bound

Flow refers to the degree of resistance that the body experiences while moving. The flow of a movement maybe classified as either *freely* or *bound*. For example, water streaming from a faucet flows free without interruption or interference. However, if you put your hand over the faucet to block or stop its stream you would bind its flow.

A free-flowing movement is spontaneous and efficient and results in the organic and authentic expression of feeling. A bound flowing movement, by contrast, is distorted and inefficient. Bound flow manifests itself in complex patterns of muscular holding. On one hand, an impulse to express a thought and feeling prompts the body to move in an outward direction, while a desire to repress the thought and feeling pulls the body in an inward direction. The result is a type of physical turmoil that reflects an individual literally pushing and pulling in two different directions. Just as rivers do not attempt to stop their water from moving downstream and wind does not try to stop itself from blowing, human beings are not designed for bound flow.

In daily discourse, context and purpose should determine the flow of the body's movement. Free-flowing movements are rewarding, desirable, and most certainly preferred, to be encouraged in life and certainly in actor training. However, occasionally binding the flow can be a useful method for making an important point or a gracious social survival tool. In negative social situations, sometimes the best approach is to simply "put up and shut up." In moderation, the regulation of an impulse can serve the greater good. However, chronic muscular holding often reflects a type of clinical depression that should ideally be treated by a trained psychologist. Similarly, free-flowing, impulsive, spontaneous actions can be violent and uncontrollable actions; they may be dynamic and exciting but are not always useful. The explosive young man who has just run his fist through the wall and busted the furniture while screaming bloody murder is doing nothing to solve his problems or to create positive alternatives to an already negative situation. Ultimately, useful and rewarding expression is not inwardly repressive or outwardly violent, but reflects a skillful coordination of muscular effort that is genuine, dynamic, and satisfying.

Exploring on Your Own

To gain a clearer understanding of the major properties of an expressive action—energy, orientation, size, progression, and flow—retrieve a book (real or imagined) from a high shelf. Repeat the action of retrieving the book several times. Allow the action to have a clearly delineated beginning, middle, and end: the initiation (agitation: wanting the book); the development (action: retrieving the book); and the resolution (satisfaction: having the book).

Now repeat the physical task several more times, exploring each of the major physical properties of an expressive action:

- *Energy: Charge/Release.* The act of reaching for the book provides the necessary power—charge. Bringing the book down from the shelf reverses the process—release.
- *Orientation: Contact/Withdraw.* An outward orientation directs you toward the book. Bringing the book down from the shelf reverses the process and results in an inward orientation.
- *Size: Expand/Contract.* Elongating and unbending various body joints makes it possible to reach the book. Contracting and bending various body joints brings the book downward so it may be held and read.
- *Progression: Center/Periphery.* Ideally, the process of retrieving the book should comprise a sequential journey of uninterrupted action from the center (pelvis) to the periphery (upward into the rib cage, shoulders, head, arms, and hands and downward through the legs, knees, ankles, and feet).
- *Flow: Free/Bound.* Begin by binding your flow. Notice how muscular tension interrupts and interferes with the efficiency of the action. Now, rest for a moment and then repeat the reaching ac-

tion, allowing the entire process to flow freely. Release any tensions that inhibit fluidity, grace, and economy.

Become aware how each of these major physical properties contributes to the structure of the physical task.

Repeat the above exploration with other simple (real or imagined) physical tasks:

Tying your shoe	Opening and closing a door
Yawning	Watching a plane fly overhead
Buttoning a jacket	Changing a lightbulb

Ideally all expressive actions, in some form or other, charge and release, contact and withdraw, expand and contract, in a sequential journey from the center of the body to the periphery in an uninterrupted and free-flowing manner. However, as you may have discovered in the exercises above, different expressive actions organize the expressive cycle in different ways. For example, some expressive actions charge before they release, while others release before they charge; some contact before they withdraw, while others withdraw before they contact; and so on. The wavelike action of the expressive cycle is a flexible structure capable of a great many modifications, adaptations, and ebbs and flows. Just as no two moments of life are repeatable, no two waves of the expressive cycle and no two expressive actions are ever the same.

Learning to participate with the ebb and flow of the expressive cycle is not something we necessarily teach the body to do but rather something we allow the body to do naturally without interruption or interference. The brain has been hardwired through years of evolutionary history to instinctively inform the body how to charge and release, to contact and withdraw, to expand and contract, to move outward from the center to the periphery, and even to flow freely. This process is natural and innate.

Minor Physical Properties of an Expressive Action

The minor physical properties of an expressive action—direction, speed, weight, control, and focus—describe additional conditions, factors, or circumstances that affect the quality and character of the action and play a secondary yet important role in further defining it.

Direction: Direct/Indirect
Direction refers to the relative straight or curved quality of an action. For example, *to scold* may be classified as a direct expressive action, *to fidget,* an indirect one.

Speed: Fast/Slow
Speed refers to the relative rate or pace of an action. For example, *to scurry* may be classified as a fast expressive action, *to plod,* a slow one.

Weight: Heavy/Light
Weight refers to the relative degree of lightness and heaviness of an action. For example, *to sulk* may be classified as a heavy expressive action, *to tiptoe,* a light one.

Control: Stable/Unstable
Control refers to the relative degree of stability or instability of an action. For example, *to stand your ground* may be classified as a stable expressive action, *to swagger,* an unstable one.

Focus: Sharp/Diffused
Focus refers to the relative degree of ocular (eye) intensity of an action. For example, *to stare* may be classified as a sharp expressive action, *to daydream,* a diffused one.

Exploring on Your Own

Select an expressive action from the list below:

to beg	to warn	to apologize
to promise	to scold	to praise

Compose a simple but flexible piece of text for the selected expressive action. (For example, for the expressive action *to promise* you might compose, "I will never tell another lie.") Play your expressive action several times while delivering the piece of text. Rest. Repeat your expressive action while exploring each of the minor properties of an expressive action sequentially: direct/indirect, fast/slow, heavy/light, stable/unstable, sharp/diffused. Become aware of the manner in which each of these minor properties affects the quality and character of the expressive action. Repeat using the other expressive actions listed above or other expressive actions of your own choosing.

The Expressive Continuum

For convenience and practicality, each of the physical properties of an expressive action can be thought of as existing on a continuum (see Figure 3.2). Each of the ten physical properties (energy, orientation, size, progression, flow, direction, speed, weight, control, and focus) exists in varying degrees in every expression action depending on the quality and character of the thought and feeling being expressed. For example, certain expressive actions are more charged than others, some may have a stronger point of contact, others might be more expansive, fast, direct, sharp, or stable. Regardless of the degree, it is important to remember that what expands must eventually contract, that what charges must ultimately be released, that a period of contact will be followed by a period of withdrawal, that an individual moving fast will eventually slow down, that a sharp focus will eventually become more diffused.

The physical properties of an expressive action are the essential building blocks of emotional expression—the raw materials that make the expression of feeling possible. *Fast* has a different emotional mean-

EXPRESSIVE CONTINUUM	
PROPERTY	**SENSORY ELEMENTS**
Energy	Charge ◄ – – – – – – – – – – – – – – ► Release
Orientation	Contact ◄ – – – – – – – – – – – – – ► Withdraw
Size	Expand ◄ – – – – – – – – – – – – – ► Contract
Progression	Center ◄ – – – – – – – – – – – – – ► Periphery
Flow	Free ◄ – – – – – – – – – – – – – – ► Bound
Direction	Direct ◄ – – – – – – – – – – – – – ► Indirect
Speed	Fast ◄ – – – – – – – – – – – – – – ► Slow
Weight	Light ◄ – – – – – – – – – – – – – ► Heavy
Control	Stable ◄ – – – – – – – – – – – – – ► Unstable
Focus	Sharp ◄ – – – – – – – – – – – – – ► Diffused

Figure 3.2 Expressive Continuum

ing from *slow*, *heavy* a different emotional meaning from *light*, *direct* a different emotional meaning from *indirect*. Different feelings are expressed by integrating the physical properties in different ways. For example, the expressive action *to mope* typically mingles *release, withdraw, indirect,* and *slow* movements. The expressive action *to pester*, by contrast, typically mingles *charge, contact, direct,* and *fast* movements.

An expressive action can be revealed in an infinite number of ways—actors with the most physical dexterity have the greatest expressive potential. Integrating and organizing the physical property of the expressive action is like mixing paint on a palette. When skillfully combined they can reveal or express almost anything. However, just as the unskilled mixing of paint ultimately results in undifferentiated shades of brown and gray, a poor mixing of physical properties can result in the undifferentiated expression of thought and feeling.

Additionally, the physical properties that make up an expressive action are not limited to bodily movement but should be applied to the voice as well. In playing an integrated expressive action, any physical shift in the body—*speed, weight, flow, focus, direction*—should ideally result in a corresponding shift in the pitch, resonance, inflection, and intonation of the actor's voice.

The physical properties of an expressive action reflect broad categories of sensation that assist in classifying and articulating our feelings. Consequently, they can only be used to describe an expressive action that we see or experience. We cannot take a specific emotion such as sadness, joy, anger, or frustration and insist that this particular feeling is always *slow, heavy, direct, charged,* or *sharp*. Fortunately, feelings will not sit still for this type of pedantic analysis.

However, for purposes of instruction, the list below identifies emotional states commonly associated with each of the physical properties that make up the expressive continuum. Because classifying any emotion is arbitrary and random, the list is general, broad, inexact, theoretical, and in no way definitive. It merely illustrates the essential link between physical sensation and emotional experience. It may also provide a deeper understanding of the terminology used in the expressive continuum.

- *Charge:* spirited, energetic, lively, animated, forceful, intense.
- *Release:* easygoing, serene, relaxed, lethargic, sluggish, lackadaisical.

- *Contact:* sociable, involved, outgoing, intrusive, extroverted, interfering.
- *Withdraw:* introspective, reflective, contemplative, unsociable, distant, detached.
- *Expand:* welcoming, accessible, available, overreaching, intrusive, meddlesome.
- *Contract:* intimate, confidential, private, insignificant, diminutive, repressive.
- *Center:* solid, stable, authentic, immovable, settled, static.
- *Periphery:* versatile, adaptable, lighthearted, superficial, flighty, frivolous.
- *Free:* liberated, spontaneous, natural, impulsive, irrepressible, imprudent.
- *Bound:* cautious, circumspect, prudent, repressed, controlled, inhibited.
- *Direct:* clear, assiduous, straightforward, abrupt, curt, blunt.
- *Indirect:* versatile, affable, flexible, erratic, wishy-washy, disingenuous.
- *Fast:* swift, smart, efficient, impulsive, hasty, reckless.
- *Slow:* careful, thorough, prudent, lazy, slow-witted, sluggish.
- *Heavy:* solid, serious, solemn, sullen, glum, depressed.
- *Light:* cheerful, lighthearted, optimistic, flighty, giddy, frivolous.
- *Stable:* secure, solid, steadfast, stubborn, strong-willed, bullheaded.
- *Unstable:* spontaneous, variable, fluctuating, unsteady, dizzy, shaky.
- *Sharp:* penetrating, cutting, acerbic, shrill, strident, harsh.
- *Diffused:* vague, distant, mysterious, dull, fuzzy, confusing.

There is nothing intrinsically positive or negative about any of these emotional states. There is a time to be animated and a time to be distant, a time to be interfering and a time to be detached, a time to be accessible and a time to be confidential, a time for stability and a time for adaptability, a time for impulsivity and a time for caution. Similarly, there is a time to be fast and a time to be slow, a time to be indirect and a time to be direct, and so on.

Exploring on Your Own

Select a physical property from the expressive continuum (light, withdrawn, expansive, bound, etc.). Explore the selected physical property as you walk around the room. For example, if you selected *slow*, begin to move around the room slowly. Allow the physical action to develop into an imagined mental and emotional experience. When this level of physical, mental, and emotional integration has been achieved, you should answer the question "What are you doing?" Possible answers include *sneaking, accusing, turning the other cheek, standing my ground, staring someone down, minding my own business, daydreaming,* any language you can think of to describe the expressive action. The exact language is immaterial as long as it is descriptive of an integrated physical action that contains or reveals thought and feeling. Repeat the exploration with numerous other physical properties.

Physical Properties of an Expressive Action Applied

The following critiques of an actor's performance are based upon a practical understanding of the major properties of an expressive action.

- Your expressive actions seem undercharged for the high stakes and risky behavior that your character is making in this scene. You seem to lack the physical and psychological energy and vitality demanded by the scene.
- Your physical tensions disallow your character to participate with the release of emotional, mental, and physical energies that are essential to the organic and spontaneous expression of genuine feeling.
- Your expressive actions lack a clearly defined beginning, middle, and end.
- You seem unable to find clearly definable points of contact with which to direct your physical, vocal, mental, and emotional energies. What specifically in each moment of this scene is your character making contact with?
- Your character seems trapped in a state of emotional and physical withdrawal that is indulgent, manipulative, and seemingly despondent. Where does your character want to reach out into the environment to change it or shape it?

- You seem to interrupt the release phase of the expressive cycle. You are working too hard. Can you find places to do less and simply participate with the passive phase of the expressive action?
- Physical tensions in your body interrupt your character's ability to freely expand and contract.
- In binding your flow, you bind the thought and feeling attempting to be expressed.
- You initiate all of your expressive actions on the periphery of the body. By starting on the outside of the action, you lose the essential deep connection with your center. This leads to a type of mugging, indicating, miming, and manipulation of the body that distorts organic and integrated expression.

Furthermore, the minor properties of expressive action (*direction, speed, weight, control,* and *focus*) provide additional objective and practical directives for critiquing an actor's performance.

Integrating Voice and Body

Traditionally, voice and body training has been a somewhat negative business, focused on fixing problems in specific parts of the body: shallow breathing, a tight jaw, held shoulders, a misaligned spine, lazy articulators, wobbly legs, a weak center, and so on. An unexpected by-product of this *part-by-part approach* is often the development of a less-than-healthy relationship with the body. Invariably when one part of the body is singled out and chastised, a negative relationship with that part develops. This only serves to further disenfranchise the pesky part and makes the desired integration all the more difficult. Psychologist James I. Kepner (1993) states:

> We do not so easily get rid of parts of ourselves merely by unlearning them. Worse, however, is the possibility of so overlearning the new, good habit that the original conflict becomes inaccessible beneath a thick layer of secondary repression. I have seen this repeatedly in devotees of various training arts, such as dance, athletics (particularly weight lifting), and the martial arts. Such people have often so assiduously worked to counter their bad habits that the original feelings and expressions are driven far below the surface. These clients have to spend much time undoing their overlearned *good* habits before they can restore connection with the self-expressions that led to the tensions and distorted postural holdings. (63)

Unfortunately, we do not learn to express ourselves better by gaining control of these seemingly uncooperative parts. The ability to coordinate the hand, head, eye, leg, arm, breath, voice, lips, and tongue in the context of fluid human expression is a highly complex process that cannot be tackled piecemeal. Fixing a problem part of the body in isolation does not necessarily ensure that the part will work correctly during the significantly more complex coordination of the whole person required for integrated expression. Skills learned in isolation often remain isolated.

What is needed is an integrated approach to voice and body training that simultaneously trains the whole body for the fluid expression of thought and feeling. But integration cannot be achieved by simply placing the *voice on top of the body* or the *body on top of the voice*. The solution is more complex than simply combining arbitrarily selected vocal exercises with arbitrarily selected movement exercises. Ideally, the synthesis should create a fluid and seamless technique.

This fluidity and seamlessness can be found in examining the physical properties of an expressive action—energy: charge/release; orientation: contact/withdraw; size: expand/contract; progression: center/periphery; flow: free/bound. In Chapters 5 through 7, these physical properties are applied directly to movement, breath, and voice training. The result is a highly specialized type of actor training rooted in the act of expression itself, thereby eliminating the need to learn a different set of principles for movement training, another set for breath training, a third set for voice training, and a fourth set for acting training. Voice and body training modeled on expressive action builds important skills in alignment, breathing, resonance, and range, yes, but it simultaneously prepares the actor to play expressive actions. It's the synthesis we're looking for.

Body Structure

The purpose of voice and body training is not merely to improve posture, breath support, vocal quality, and articulation—important skills for sure—but to develop a flexible body structure. James I. Kepner (1993) defines body structure as "the way we shape ourselves and have been shaped by our life experience." Body structure refers to the organization of the whole body—bones, muscles, tissue, organs, and all. Ideally, a person with a flexible body structure possesses the necessary vocal and physical dexterity to shape any thought or feeling, no matter how powerful or intense, into meaningful expressive action. In a flexible body structure, the right muscles are always engaged at the right time to perform the right action. Barring biological defect, everyone shares a universal body structure that is by design intended to be flexible and adaptable.

Children have flexible bodies. Childhood is characterized by great physical and vocal flexibility, spontaneity, and vitality. Over time, however, the relatively limited and repetitive physical demands of contemporary adult living cause the once flexible body of the child to lose its dexterity, adaptability, and even its spontaneity and vitality. In time, certain physical and vocal patterns become frozen and fixed in the musculature of the body, limiting the possibility of varied and flexible expression.

In today's sedentary culture, a relatively fixed body structure is commonly acquired as early as adolescence. Fixed body structures are characterized by modes of expression that:

1. Are consistently used over time,
2. Are automatic or involuntary, and
3. Can be modified only through conscious effort.

Fixed body structures develop for three reasons:

1. Chronic muscular tension,
2. Imbalances in strength and flexibility, and/or
3. A static and inflexible personality.

Because the actor may be called upon to express any and every human emotion, a technical means of maintaining a flexible body is essential. The goal of good training is to develop a strong, flexible, free, coordinated body.

Actual Versus Ideal

The road to fluid and flexible expression is a complex human journey. It involves exploration, discovery, discipline, self-respect, and patience. This journey begins with the belief that all human beings have the potential for dynamic, varied, and flexible expression that is capable of communicating every feeling, nuance, attitude, mood, and desire that can be experienced by the species. It requires the actor to imagine an ideal world—the possibility of perfect expression not limited by force of habit, physical deficiencies, psychological imbalances, personal idiosyncrasies, or immaturity.

The actor in training should begin focusing not on what *is* but rather on what *ought* or *could* be if the conditions are right. It is important to emphasize the *possible* rather than the *actual*. Ideally, the actor should not focus on what is *wrong* with the body or the voice but on how the body and voice are designed to work *right*. Actors need to envision themselves in an ideal light—without the squeaky or husky voice, the awkward and gangly arms, the spindly and unstable legs, the tense jaw or shoulders, the fear of deep feeling or large expression. The pessimist is quick to question whether the ideal is reachable, easily conceding that certain limitations may be difficult to overcome. However, actors interested in improving must remain optimistic. A negative approach limits growth and impedes progress.

This is not to suggest that a positive attitude will solve all problems at the expense of hard work. Indeed, the actor's road to free and varied expression can be long and hard. Unfortunately, not all actors experience growth at the same rate. It can take as long as three years to significantly reorganize one's body structure. Even then, some deep-seated patterns and tensions are often not completely resolved. The mistake of the pessimist is to see the glass half empty. To embrace the ideal (and indeed technique itself), the actor must always maintain a positive outlook, celebrating the potential for and the process of change—slow or fast, steady or intermittent, accelerated or seemingly arrested.

Each actor brings to the training a unique set of strengths and weaknesses. Consequently, each person should move at his or her own pace. A healthy way of working requires maintaining an acceptable comfort level. A responsible approach strikes a healthy balance between challenging the body without abusing it—between pushing and pampering, disciplining and nurturing. Personality plays a strong role in the manner in which each individual approaches the work. Regardless of a person's particular disposition, there is a time to rest and a time to push ahead. The best learners seem to make these choices intuitively, never injuring or hurting themselves, while simultaneously reaching, exploring, and conquering new and uncharted territory.

The body is a creature of habit. It likes to do what it has been doing. Often when we ask the body to do something new, it puts up a struggle. Mental discipline, willpower, commitment, and physical tenacity are important for development and change. What often appears difficult and uncomfortable at first, with time becomes easy, familiar, and rewarding.

Movement

Movement is essentially a series of weight shifts made possible because the human body is a segmented structure (see Figure 5.1). Each body segment is connected to another body segment by a series of joints. When a joint is bent or flexed, lengthened or extended, rotated or turned, the body's weight is redistributed. Pointing the foot, bending the knee, rotating the head, waving the wrist, shifting the hips, bending the elbow, are all examples of weight shifts. We learn to move well when we learn to shift our weight well.

There are two types of weight shifts: *isolated* and *integrated*. Isolated weight shifts involve moving one body segment at a time. They occur when one segment of the body is *set apart* from the other body segments and moved alone or independently. Tapping the foot, shaking the head, and shrugging the shoulders are examples of isolated weight shifts. By contrast, integrated weight shifts occur when multiple body segments move together in unison and harmony. The vast majority of all human movement involves some type of integrated weight shift. Picking up a pencil off the floor, opening a window, hugging a friend, or simply walking all involve the integrated movement of many body segments.

Moving one part of the body is decidedly simpler than moving the whole body. Isolated weight shifts are therefore the simplest movements the body can make. Because integrated weight shifts require a

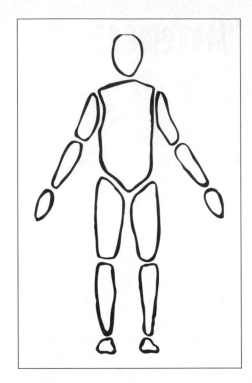

Figure 5.1 Segmented Structure

more sophisticated redistribution of body weight, movement training typically concentrates on integrated weight shifts. Integrated weight shifts are central to the expression of powerful and important thoughts and feelings. We feel with our whole body, not in isolated sections, parts, or segments. An integrated weight shift corresponds directly to a shift in thought and feeling. Larger thoughts and feelings are expressed through larger weight shifts, smaller thoughts and feelings through smaller weight shifts.

Exploring on Your Own

Wave hello to an imaginary friend. Like any movement, this is not possible without a weight shift, either isolated or integrated.

First, use an isolated weight shift. Keeping your pelvis, torso, shoulders, and head relatively uninvolved, lift only your arm and hand

and wave hello to your friend. Your goal is to isolate or separate the action of your arm and hand from the rest of your body. The waving action should happen only in the appendages. Your arm and hand move independently and in isolation with seemingly no connection to the rest of your body. Repeat several times.

Now, wave hello to your friend using an integrated weight shift. Allow the action to begin deep in the center of your body. Feel your whole body expand. You should experience the waving action from the soles of your feet to the top of your head. Stand on your tiptoes. Jump up and down. Allow your entire shoulder and torso to participate in the waving action. Repeat several times. The larger movement associated with an integrated weight shift corresponds to a greater sense of commitment, intensity, and feeling.

Movement Progression: Center/Periphery

The natural progression of a movement begins in the pelvis—the geographical center of the body (see Figure 5.2)—and flows outward to the periphery into the arms, legs, hands, feet, and head. Three factors make the pelvis the ideal place to initiate movement:

1. It has the heaviest bones. Thus this body segment assumes primary responsibility for moving other, lighter body segments.
2. It has the largest joints. Stress and strain on the smaller joints of the body are eliminated when the pelvis initiates and coordinates movement.
3. It has the strongest muscles. Efficiency dictates that the strongest muscles should do the lion's share of the work.

It's natural and logical that a weight shift in the pelvis would be an ideal place to begin physical activity. Common sense suggests that leading with the pelvis is more efficient, pleasant, and advantageous than leading with the shoulders, head, rib cage, legs, or feet. No matter which direction we desire to move—bending down to touch the toes or reaching the hands and arms up over the head—the journey is more fluid, efficient, and integrated when the action is initiated from the pelvis.

The pelvis is somewhat like the engine of a train; when it moves, all the other body segments, like boxcars, follow its lead. Consequently, the pelvis is instrumental in coordinating the action of the legs

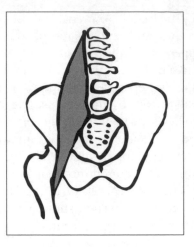

Figure 5.2 Pelvic Center

and feet with the action of the torso, arms, and head. When initiated correctly, a weight shift in the pelvis ensures that the upper half of the body moves in concert and harmony with the lower half of the body. The result is integrated, functional efficiency.

An integrated weight shift in the pelvis progresses sequentially in a wavelike action to the periphery, through the torso, arms, head, hands, legs, and feet. This wavelike action proceeds simultaneously in both an upward and downward direction:

1. Upper-body sequence: pelvis + rib cage + head.
2. Lower-body sequence: pelvis + knee + ankle + foot.

While the pelvis provides the raw power and support necessary for movement, the periphery of the body—the arms, hands, legs, feet, and head—serve the important function of guiding and directing the movement of the body in space. Nevertheless, this guiding and directing action is secondary to the primary action occurring in the pelvis. Stress and strain occur when the muscles and the bones located on the periphery of the body are wrongly engaged to do the strenuous work that should ideally be performed by the pelvis. The right muscles must be asked to perform the right tasks. When working to improve the way the body moves, it is important to allow the periphery of the body to be carried and supported from the pelvis: the center moves and the periphery follows. This releases unnecessary tensions in the body that interrupt integrated and efficient movement.

The Thigh Socket

The prerequisite for initiating a movement from the pelvis is strength, flexibility, and freedom in the thigh socket—essentially the hip joint, the point where the upper leg is inserted into the pelvis. This joint is commonly referred to as the *ball-and-socket joint*. The process of re-structuring the body's movement patterns begins by initiating all movement with a weight shift in the pelvis. In practice, this involves directing one's attention to the place where the ball and socket meet and encouraging movement from this most important central hinge. In the beginning, this centered weight shift can be obvious, over-pronounced, and laborious, because muscles located deep in the center of the body can be difficult to coordinate. However, with time and skill, inefficient weight shifts give way to smaller, subtler, even semi-conscious ones. Eventually it is possible to initiate movement from the pelvis with such subtlety and economy that it is almost imperceptible.

Developing a sophisticated connection with the thigh socket is an essential first step in learning to integrate the action of the breath and the action of the voice with the action of the body. Because a movement initiated from the pelvis sets the whole body in motion, the action of the breath and the action of the voice are directly in-fluenced and shaped by the action of the pelvis. This integrated interplay between moving, breathing, and speaking is essential to in-tegrated expression.

Exploring on Your Own

Begin by sitting comfortably on the edge of a traditional chair. Allow your "sit" bones to release comfortably into the seat of the chair. Al-low both feet to rest securely and stably on the floor. Allow your hands to rest comfortably on your knees. Allow your spine to float into a vertical and upright position without slouching downward or reach-ing upward. Focusing your attention on the ball-and-socket joint, gently rotate your pelvis to the right and then to the left. Repeat this action several times. Allow your upper and lower body to cooperate passively with the movement of your pelvis. If your body is at ease and relatively free of tension, this centered weight shift in your pelvis will reverberate sequentially through your whole body—upward into the torso and head, and downward through the legs and feet. Release any tensions that interrupt this integrated and full-bodied action. Enjoy the deep connection to your movement center. Rest.

Now, raise both arms outward at about shoulder height. Do not lock your elbows or wrists. Once again, gently rotate your pelvis from side to side. Allow your shoulders, arms, and hands to respond to the movement of your pelvis. Your arms will move subtly in an alternating forward and backward direction in concert with the weight shift in your pelvis. Sense the weight of your shoulders, arms, and hands being carried and supported by your spine and pelvis. Rest and repeat.

Movement Size: Expand/Contract

Modifications or changes in the body's "size" are created through the bending and unbending of various joints, which results in relative changes in the degree of expansion and contraction experienced in the body. Ideally, each joint of the body should enjoy a free and uninterrupted range of motion so that all the joints can expand and contract efficiently. For this to occur, the muscles of the body must be both strong and flexible. Weak muscles have difficulty contracting; tight muscles have difficulty expanding.

In general, the average person's wrists, ankles, elbows, knees, and feet are strong and flexible enough to perform a wide array of physical actions. It is relatively easy to expand and contract the smaller joints of the body. Consequently, movement training focuses primarily on learning to expand and contract the spine efficiently.

The expansion and contraction of the spine is the largest movement the body makes and is integral to almost every smaller movement that the body makes. Individuals with a strong and flexible spine invariably experience adequate levels of strength and flexibility in the rest of the muscles and joints of the body. When the spine is expanding and contracting properly, the other muscles and joints in the body tend to follow its lead.

In movement training, the spine is often addressed in the context of good or bad posture. Consequently, the ability to hold the spine vertical and upright is often celebrated at the expense of its other important movement properties. The spine is not simply designed to keep the body erect and upright but to expand and contract—to bend and rotate, twist and turn, with great flexibility and in a variety of combinations.

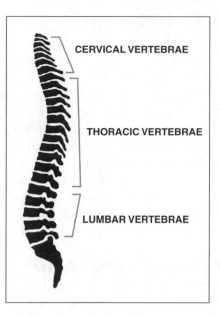

CERVICAL VERTEBRAE

THORACIC VERTEBRAE

LUMBAR VERTEBRAE

Figure 5.3 Spine

One reason expanding and contracting the spine can be so diffi-cult is that the architecture of the spine is complex and generally misunderstood. The most common misconception is to view the spine as a stiff, inflexible structure like that of a broomstick or a metal rod. Rather, the spine is a series of connected curved bones (vertebrae) forming a series of twenty-four interconnected joints that allow the spine to expand and contract (see Figure 5.3).

The spine is designed to transfer the weight of the head, shoul-ders, arms, and rib cage downward into the pelvis. This downward transfer of weight is facilitated by the vertebrae of the spine, which become larger and stronger as they progress lower and lower into the body. The pelvis—the base of the spine—is strategically positioned to support and carry the weight of the entire upper body. Its bowl-like shape serves as a type of cradle, which not only supports and carries the weight of the upper body but also absorbs and cushions shock and stress during strenuous activity.

When the spine is expanded (upright and vertical), the weight of the upper body is transferred into the pelvis through a relatively straight vertical pathway. However, as the spine contracts, this straight vertical pathway becomes curved or rounded. The ability to expand

and contract the spine without interrupting the fluid transfer of the weight of the upper body downward into the pelvis is essential to fluid and efficient movement.

When attempting to improve the use of the spine, the essential question is not, "Where should I place or hold my spine in space?" but, "How should I move my spine through space?" Individuals with the skill to move the spine in all its possible dimensions have good posture and alignment naturally. Rigorous movement disciplines such as dance, the martial arts, and many sports spend little time discussing vertical alignment or posture. The physical demands of these disciplines indirectly improve the alignment of the spine. A spine that can expand and contract efficiently and economically—that can bend, turn, twist, and rotate—finds itself in *correct alignment* by default.

Creasing and De-creasing the Thigh Socket

Essential to being able to expand and contract the spine efficiently is the ability to crease and de-crease the thigh socket, the body's central hinge, a concept similar to that of folding and unfolding a sheet of paper (see Figure 5.4). When a piece of paper is folded in half, a crease is formed in the center. Similarly, as the upper body folds over the lower body, a crease is created in the thigh socket (the center of the body). When we crease, or bend, from the thigh socket, the whole spine *contracts*. As we de-crease, or unbend, from the thigh socket, the whole spine *expands*. Learning to crease and de-crease the thigh socket efficiently ensures that the spine will expand and contract freely and

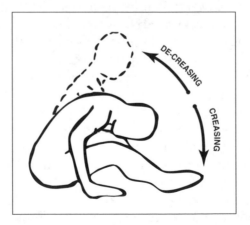

Figure 5.4 Creasing/De-creasing

naturally—that all the interconnected vertebrae will move in unison and harmoniously with one another, creating a fluid and uninterrupted pathway of movement and support.

Exploring on Your Own

Begin in a seated position on the floor. Bend your legs at the knees and allow the soles of your feet to touch each other so that your legs and feet form a diamond shape. Allow your spine to float into a vertical and upright position without slouching downward or reaching upward. Initiate a looping action by creasing and de-creasing your thigh socket several times. Creasing your thigh socket loops your pelvis, rib cage, and head downward over your legs and feet—a contraction. Decreasing your thigh socket loops your pelvis, rib cage, and head upward away from your legs and feet—an expansion. The looping action is performed in a fluid and circular pattern, not as an isolated up-and-down movement in which the upper body is systematically raised and lowered over the legs and feet. Encourage the sensation of your upper body being suspended from your pelvis and hovering out over your legs and feet rather than collapsing downward toward the floor. A sense of freedom and ease in the thigh socket facilitates the fluid expansion and contraction of the spine. Repeat this looping action several more times.

Movement Energy: Charge/Release

A weight shift is not possible without a corresponding building up and letting go of energy. The sensation associated with building up energy is a *charge*. The sensation associated with letting this energy go is a *release*. The terms *charge* and *release* must not be confused with the more common terms *tension* and *relaxation*.

The physical experience of a *charge* is very different from the physical experience of *tension*. When the body experiences an increased charge, the buildup of energy is spontaneous, involuntary, and generally infectious. It travels from the center of the body outward to the periphery in uninterrupted waves of excitement. Tension, on the other hand, interrupts spontaneity and stifles the free flow of energy in the body. Tension is caused by the conscious or unconscious tightening of muscles. Unlike a charge, which is a full-bodied experience, tension is typically a localized and isolated phenomenon. Tension can occur almost anywhere—the head, shoulders, hands, neck, jaw, forehead, and feet. A charge is a type of positive body energy that facilitates expressive action; tension is a type of negative body energy that inhibits or blocks expressive action.

Similarly, relaxation refers to an overall decrease in the level of energy in the whole body. Relaxation is commonly associated with sleepiness, lethargy, and heaviness. Release, on the other hand, is not so much a condition, state, or mood, but a letting go of the prerequisite physical, emotional, and mental energy that makes movement possible. Release is actually a byproduct of the charge. When the body charges, by design it eventually must release. Release is essentially a *reaction* to the prior charging action of the body. It is not the generalized sensation of letting go experienced after a hard day's work, when on vacation, while sipping a cocktail or having a massage, but a phase in the cyclical process of an integrated and organized movement. An individual in a very relaxed state and an individual bustling with boundless energy are both charging and releasing in relatively equal measure as they respond to the ebb and flow of life.

Working With and Against the Forces of Gravity

Learning to move efficiently involves organizing a charging and releasing action in the pelvis. This requires learning to work *with* and *against* the forces of gravity. When the pelvis pushes the body up and away from the earth, the body experiences a charge. Reciprocally, when the pelvis yields and gives in to gravity, the body experiences a release. When we move efficiently, a *charge* propels or pushes the body up and away from the earth on a wave of momentous energy. After the charging action has run its course, the body passively releases and moves in a downward direction back down toward the earth.

Efficient movement is a finely orchestrated dance between the forces of conscious muscle action (charge) and passive muscle action (release). In certain movement patterns our body *charges* before it *releases,* and in other movement patterns our body *releases* before it *charges.* Regardless of the order of the charging and releasing action, in every phrase of movement there is time for activity and passivity, doing and nondoing, action and inaction—charge and release.

Exploring on Your Own

Throwing an imaginary punch is a movement that *charges* before it *releases.* Typically, a good fighter throws a punch from the pelvis, using the weight of the entire body to knock out his opponent. Throw a pretend punch several times. Taking a few steps forward as the punch is thrown is essential to experiencing a full-bodied charge and release in the pelvis. Notice as you throw the punch how your body charges up and away from the earth before it releases downward toward the earth. Repeat this punching action several times. Focus on the contrasting sensation of charge and release created by the action of the pelvis.

Rolling an imaginary bowling ball down the alley is a movement that *releases* before it *charges*. Typically, a good bowler initiates the rolling action from the pelvis, using the weight of the entire body to propel the ball down the alley. Taking a few steps forward as the ball leaves your hand is essential to experiencing a full-bodied release and charge in the pelvis. Notice as you throw the ball how your body releases downward toward the earth before it charges up and away from the earth. Repeat this throwing action several more times. Focus your attention on the contrasting sensation of release and charge created by the movement of the pelvis.

Movement Orientation: Contact/Withdraw

Orientation refers to the directional forces that motivate the movement of the individual in the environment. A forward and advancing outward movement reflects an individual in *contact* with the environment. Reciprocally, an inward and retreating movement reflects an individual *withdrawing* from the environment. Ideally, an individual makes contact with the environment to fulfill physical or psychological needs and withdraws when these needs have been satisfied. Because the body cannot move in an inward and outward direction at the same time, the efficiency and authenticity of any movement is improved when the mover has a clear understanding of when the body makes contact with the environment and when the body withdraws from the environment. Identifying the logical pattern of contact and withdrawal is an essential first step when analyzing the structure of any human movement.

Movement Flow: Free/Bound

Responsible movement training fosters free-flowing patterns of movement that create an ideal physical environment for the expression of thought and feeling. The free flow of energy in the body produces an expansion in the body's connective tissue. This allows for greater flexibility, dexterity, and range of motion in all the joints.

When the flow of energy in the body is *bound*, muscular tension inhibits the body's movement. The "held" part of the body is unable to participate freely in the expression of thought and feeling. Bound flow is a repressive or regulatory action that distorts natural and spontaneous behavior. The most common muscular tensions that bind the body's flow are:

- Contracting the back of the neck
- Clenching the jaw
- Tightening the tongue
- Constricting the throat
- Lifting the shoulders and rib cage
- Tensing the hands and fingers
- Holding in the muscles of the abdomen
- Locking the pelvis
- Tightening the buttocks
- Gripping the upper legs (quadriceps)
- Locking the knees
- Clenching or gripping the fingers or toes

When working to free held parts of the body, the goal is not simply to relax the held part but rather to encourage the held part to participate in the larger charging and releasing, contacting and withdrawing, expanding and contracting action that is occurring in the whole body. The goal is always integration rather than isolation.

Breath

The breath provides the framework and the foundation for sound. Efficient and coordinated breathing paves the way for a strong, free, resonant voice. The breath is a type of highway on which the voice travels. The role of the breath is to stabilize and support the voice of the speaker. The breath is being supported properly when an appropriate degree of pressure in the breath stream vibrates the vocal folds and propels the voice forward into the mouth and throat, so that the lips, teeth, tongue, and jaw can shape the sound into meaningful words, phrases, and sentences. If the pressure in the breath stream is insufficient, weak, or erratic, the voice loses its power and support.

The purpose of breath training is to develop flexibility, dexterity, strength, control, and freedom in the muscles that make breathing possible. A telltale sign of faulty breath management is excessive muscular tension. When this occurs, the muscles of the throat, tongue, jaw, soft palate, neck, shoulders, and rib cage desperately attempt to supply, bolster, and stabilize an unsteady and weak breath stream. The body fights the breath, and the breath fights the body. Inhalation is forced, audible, and overtly muscular. Exhalation is strained, pressed, and congested.

While most people have little trouble finding adequate breath support for their voices in daily life, the rigorous demands of acting in large spaces, over long periods of time, in highly challenging physical and emotional situations, places special demands on the actor's voice. Without specialized training, the actor often strains and pushes the voice in a desperate attempt to express large and powerful feelings (or simply be heard in the back row of the theatre). Taken to extremes, this pushing and straining can lead to vocal problems requiring medical attention. Even less severe vocal stress is physically debilitating and often aesthetically unsatisfying. A voice that is pushed or forced is not only tired and strained but lacks range, subtlety, flexibility, efficiency, and a complexity of tone that is essential to the nuanced expression of thought and feeling.

Two groups of muscles make breath support possible:

1. muscles of inspiration—the breathing-in muscles;
2. muscles of expiration—the breathing-out muscles.

Typically, faulty breath support occurs for two reasons:

1. insufficient inhalation and/or
2. a poorly managed exhalation.

The primary muscle of inspiration is the diaphragm. This dome-shaped muscle located in the middle of the body separates the chest from the abdomen. The diaphragm is attached to the lungs, and during inhalation moves downward toward the abdomen. This downward movement increases the volume of the lungs, causing the air pressure in the lungs to decrease and creating a type of vacuum, which draws the breath into the lungs. Another important but secondary group of inspiratory muscles are the intercostals, which are located between the ribs and assist the diaphragm by expanding the rib cage during inhalation. The primary muscles of expiration are a group of abdominal muscles located above and below the navel on the front and the sides of the body. During active expiration, these muscles push the abdomen in, increasing the pressure in the breath stream, thus providing stability and support to the outgoing breath. (See Figure 6.1)

How the *breathing-in* and *breathing-out* muscles work together to make speech possible is a complicated scientific subject. All I can safely say here is that successful breath management involves varying degrees of activity and passivity in the muscles of inspiration and expiration. These muscles work *with* and *against* each other to stabilize the flow of the outgoing breath. Breath support is made possible by a gradual

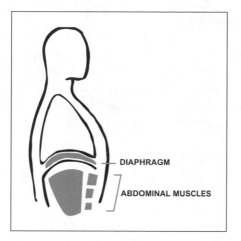

Figure 6.1 Breathing Musculature

transfer of energy from the muscles of inspiration to the muscles of expiration, creating a balance of tension, which provides just enough pressure to suspend the breath and support the tone.

Breath Progression: Center/Periphery

The breathing center is located in the middle of the belly. The natural progression of the breath flows freely from the middle of the belly outward to the periphery in all directions. An awareness of the breathing center is developed by focusing on the movement of the diaphragm, the large muscle separating the chest and the abdomen. The diaphragm descends during inhalation, causing a pronounced movement in the middle of the belly in corresponding outward and downward directions. The movement of the body during diaphragmatic breathing is similar to dropping a stone into a pool of water. The circular ripples of the water emanate most strongly from the center (the middle of the belly) and progress with less power and intensity as they move outward toward the periphery (upward into the chest and downward into the pelvis). The progression is directly related to the intensity of the thought and feeling being expressed. Smaller thoughts and feeling travel a smaller distance from the center, while larger thoughts and feelings progress further outward to the periphery.

Peripheral Breathing

Breathing that is not centered in the middle of the belly but in the upper chest is called *clavicle breathing*. In this type of breathing, the diaphragm is not initiating and coordinating the breathing action and the predominate movement in the body occurs in the upper chest near the collar bone. Breathing centered too high in the body poses numerous problems (Anderson 1977):

- *Capacity:* The muscles of the upper chest and collarbone area are too high in the body to expand the lower lungs to full capacity. Since less breath is taken in, less breath is available to support the voice.

- *Efficiency:* The muscles of the upper chest and collarbone area do not have the power or strength of the diaphragm and the abdominal muscles to coordinate the breathing action.

- *Support:* The muscles that provide breath support are primarily located in the abdomen, not the upper chest. When breathing is centered too high in the body, the ability to control and stabilize the outgoing breath is compromised.

- *Location:* When muscles in the upper chest and throat are wrongly engaged to support the voice, the action of these muscles—largely because of their close proximity to the vocal folds—interferes with the efficient functioning of the voice. Because the abdominal muscles are further away from the vocal folds, they are able to support the voice efficiently without interfering with the action of the vocal folds.

Exploring on Your Own

Panting—breathing in and out very rapidly—is a practical way to become aware of the breathing center. Because this action is quick and reflexive, it is virtually impossible to pant without engaging the diaphragm. Lie comfortably on your back. Bend your knees so that the soles of your feet make contact with the floor. Your feet should rest in an unstrained position near your buttocks. Don't let your knees collapse inward or fall outward. Allow the weight of the floor to support you. Let the abdominal muscles soften. Allow your jaw to drop so that the breath flows freely in and out of your mouth. Initiate a quick and vibrant panting action from your breathing center. Escalate the intensity of the panting for several seconds. Then let it subside naturally. (Do not hyperventilate.) The panting sequence should have a clearly defined beginning, middle, and end. Become aware of the action of the diaphragm in the middle of your belly. Observe the progression of the breath from the center to the periphery. Repeat this process two or three more times, resting in between each panting sequence.

Breath Size: Expand/Contract

The journey of the breath from the center to the periphery creates obvious changes in the size of the body. The circumference of the chest and abdomen increases as the breath enters the body and decreases as the breath leaves the body. Expansion occurs during inhalation; contraction occurs during exhalation. The skillful expansion and contraction of the body involves the coordination of the upper breathing space and the lower breathing space (see Figure 6.2). The upper breathing space begins at the collarbone and extends downward to the bottom of the breastbone. The lower breathing space begins at the base of the breastbone and extends downward to the pubic bone. However, remember that the breathing spaces extend around to the sides and the back of the body as well.

Effective breathing involves the integrated action of the upper and lower breathing spaces. In general, a greater degree of expansion should be sensed in the front of the body in the lower breathing space, because (see Figure 6.3):

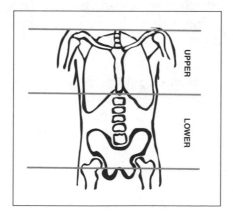

Figure 6.2 Breathing Spaces

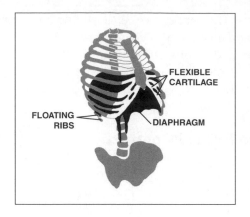

Figure 6.3 Breathing Anatomy

1. During inhalation, the diaphragm descends downward toward the pelvis, creating a greater depth of movement in the lower breathing space.

2. The ribs in the lower breathing space do not extend all the way across the front of the body as they do in the upper breathing space (the two lowest ribs are floating ribs and are not attached to the breastbone). Consequently, a soft malleable space is created in the lower breathing space that is responsive to the inward and outward movement of the breath.

3. A great portion of the front ribs in the lower breathing space are comprised of flexible cartilage and not solid bone like the ribs in the upper breathing space, allowing for a greater degree of movement in the lower breathing space.

Therefore, the most pronounced breathing action in the majority of skilled speakers and singers occurs in the front of the body in the lower breathing space.

This is not to suggest that there is no movement in the upper breathing space or on the sides and back of the body. Both the upper and lower breathing spaces must be free to move in response to the incoming and outgoing breath. Breathing is a full-bodied activity that with awareness and sensitivity can be felt from the collarbone all the way down to the pubic bone. However, a disproportionate displacement in the upper breathing space interferes with the architectural design of the body and is most probably the result of misdirected muscular effort. But care must also be taken not to push or force the breath into the lower breathing space. Most often, the lower breathing space can be accessed indirectly by releasing unnecessary tensions in the belly that inhibit the breath from dropping deeply into the body. In practice, it is better to think of taking a *complete breath* rather than a *deep breath*. This directive invites a full and adequate inhalation from the diaphragm that is never pressed or forced into the lower breathing space. Ultimately, the goal is a free and complete inhalation capable of communicating the richness of the thought and feeling being expressed.

Exploring on Your Own

Lie comfortably on your back. Bend your knees so that the soles of your feet make contact with the floor. Your feet should rest in an unstrained position near your buttocks. Don't let your knees collapse inward or fall outward. Allow the weight of the floor to support you. Let your abdominal muscles soften. Allow your jaw to drop so that your breath flows freely in and out of your mouth. Place one hand on your chest (the upper breathing space) and the other hand on your belly (the lower breathing space). (This will increase your awareness of the expansion and contraction in the upper and lower breathing spaces.) Pant quickly and vibrantly from your breathing center, as in the previous exploration. Rest. Become aware of the relative degree of expansion and contraction in your upper and lower breathing spaces. Slow the panting sequence down, taking deeper and more complete breaths. This slower and deeper breathing should no longer feel like panting but like the slower and deeper breaths you might experience after running a fifty-yard dash (minus the fatigue). Do not work too hard. Receive your breath naturally and give it away freely. Allow your inhalation and the exhalation to be relatively equal in length. Become aware of the relative degree of expansion and contraction in your upper and lower breathing spaces. Rest. Repeat this action again, this time taking even slower and deeper breaths. Once again, become aware of the relative degree of expansion and contraction in your upper and lower breathing spaces. Rest. Always take care not to hyperventilate.

Breath Energy: Charge/Release

Successful breath management involves regulating energy in the body by structuring and organizing the contrasting sensations of *charge* and *release* that regulate the rate and flow of the exhalation. This involves cultivating two distinct physical sensations while exhaling:

1. Release (the breath falls from the body).
2. Charge (the body carries the breath).

Allowing the breath to fall from the body is a simple and straight-forward method of breath management. This type of exhalation occurs when the breath *passively* leaves the body. When we breathe in this manner, no effort is made to regulate or manage the release of the outgoing breath. We simply receive a new breath in, then let the breath go. A practical way to practice this type of passive breath management is by sighing. (My understanding of the concept of a sigh of relief is deeply indebted to my initial voice training with Kristin Linklater [see Linklater 1976].) When we sigh, the breath falls from the body freely and without interruption. The body experiences this decrease in physical energy as a release: it's like blowing up a balloon and letting it go. Most important, this passive type of exhalation occurs without any assistance from the muscles of expiration. Learning to allow the breath to fall from the body involves cultivating the sensation of deep release not only in the breathing musculature but in the whole body.

Allowing the body to carry the breath is more complex. In this type of exhalation, the breath *actively* leaves the body: the rate and flow of the outgoing breath is stabilized and lengthened. A practical way to practice active exhalation is by hissing—sustaining an interrupted, continuous *sss* sound while exhaling. When breathing in this manner, the breath does not rush out passively but is actively sustained in the body. Ideally, the breath leaves the body in a coordinated and organized manner, not in erratic fits and starts. The body experiences this regulated emission of breath as a charge.

Essential to this active type of exhalation is cultivating the sensation of the whole body *carrying the breath*. Ideally, the rate at which the breath is expelled is determined by a variety of complex factors linked directly to the size and intensity of the thought or feeling being expressed.

All speech exists somewhere between *charge* and *release*. Efficient breathing requires striking the perfect balance of energy. Sometimes our speech is highly charged, sometimes it is more released, and sometimes it falls in the middle. As the body learns the varying degrees of charge and release required for various types of expression, the breathing musculature reflexively supports the voice of the speaker. When the body and the breath work together, the flow of the outgoing breath instinctively harmonizes with the movement of the body. The speaker does not have to think about releasing, regulating, or controlling the outgoing breath. The action of the body provides a structure and framework, which is transferred or telegraphed to the action of the breath. When this occurs, the breath is released, sustained, and replaced in harmony with the movement of the body without unnecessary stress or strain.

Exploring on Your Own

Stand upright with your legs about shoulder-width apart. Allow your arms to rest comfortably at your sides. Bend and unbend your knees in a comfortable plié-like action several times. Repeat. As you bend your knees, allow your breath to fall from your body. Each time you straighten your knees, receive a new breath. The falling breath should be similar to a sigh—an unvoiced *huh* sound. Allow the release of physical energy in your whole body to coordinate the release of the outgoing breath. Rest. Now take three steps forward. As you move forward, allow your body to carry the breath as you sustain a simple *sss* sound over the three-step phrase. Feel the buildup of physical energy in your whole body that lengthens and sustains the *sss* sound. Rest and repeat. Now let your breath fall from your body during four knee bends and carry your breath during four steps forward. Then try five knee bends and five steps forward, followed by six, seven, eight, perhaps more, as many as feel comfortable. Do not push or strain your breath by going beyond what you are able to support. Enjoy the contrasting sensation of the breath falling from and being carried by your body—charge and release.

Breath Orientation: Contact/Withdraw

During vocal expression, the breath travels from inside the body outside into the environment. This inner-to-outer-and-back-again journey of the breath plays a pivotal role in guiding and directing the orientation of the speaker. Contact is characterized by an outward movement of the breath; withdrawal is characterized by an inward movement of the breath. The sensations associated with withdrawal are linked directly to inhalation; the sensations associated with contact are linked directly to exhalation. Inhalation reflects a period of *inspiration*. The speaker is *inspired* by internal thoughts and feelings that have not yet been externally expressed. The contact phase occurs when the speaker shares this inspiration with the outside world.

When the natural process of contact and withdrawal is interrupted, breathing problems invariably develop. Individuals experiencing unwanted inner emotional turmoil often breathe shallowly and incompletely. By not breathing in, they hope to avoid the unpleasant feelings churning around inside them, thereby interrupting the withdrawal phase of the breath cycle. Similarly, individuals whose outer world is stressful or violent are often afraid to breathe out. By not breathing out, they hope to avoid the conflict and negativity that surrounds them, thereby interrupting the contact phase of the breath cycle.

Efficient breathing is linked directly to developing the courage and personal maturity needed to accept and deal responsibly with the host of internal and external stimuli that accompany living.

Exploring on Your Own

Lie comfortably on your back. Bend your knees so that the soles of your feet make contact with the floor. Your feet should rest in an unstrained position near your buttocks. Don't let your knees collapse inward or fall outward. Allow the weight of the floor to support you. Let your abdominal muscles soften. Allow your jaw to drop so that the breath flows freely in and out of your mouth. Observe the rise and fall of your breath for several moments. Rest. Become aware of the rising and falling action of your breath once again. Each time you receive a new breath, close your eyes and turn your attention inward—withdraw. Each time you breathe out, open your eyes and make contact with something in the room. Rest and repeat. Enjoy the contrasting sensations of contact and withdrawal associated with the outgoing and ingoing breath.

Breath Flow: Free/Bound

Free breathing is fluid, natural, flexible, adaptable, and unlabored. Bound breathing is rigid, tight, shallow, pressed, and labored. The easiest way to free the breath is to free the body by releasing unnecessary tensions that interrupt the natural action of breathing. As the body becomes freer, breathing becomes freer as well. Common spots of tension often include the jaw, lips, tongue, and throat, as well as the shoulders, rib cage, and belly. When releasing the tensions that are interrupting the freedom of the breath, take care not to overrelax the whole body. The directive to *relax* can often result in the unwanted experience of *collapse*. A drop in physical energy is invariably accompanied by a drop in mental and emotional energy. Freedom in the breathing musculature does not have to come at the expense of energy and vitality in the rest of the body. In a deeply relaxed state, the possibility of vital, active, energetic expression is severely limited. Ultimately, the actor must breathe freely when the body is alert, energized, and expressive as well as when it is released, relaxed, and restful. Remember that *tension* is a troublesome enemy, *energy* a trusted friend. Physical tensions in the body rarely need to be relaxed, only redirected into useful physical actions that help us express our thoughts and feelings.

When the breath is freed, feeling is also freed. The feeling center of the body and the breathing center of the body are both situated, more or less, in the middle of the belly. The ancient Greeks held that the diaphragm was the center of joy, laughter, grief, weeping, pride, and self-reliance. Our most powerful thoughts and feelings invariably manifest themselves in our breath. Consequently, anytime we are holding onto our feelings, we are inevitably holding our breath.

Sound

Sound vibrations begin in the larynx, or voice box, a muscle-and-cartilage structure at the top of the windpipe that houses the vocal folds. The pitch of the voice is determined largely by the action of the vocal folds. When the breath stream moves across the vocal folds, they begin to vibrate, creating the initial sound that makes speech possible—a sound similar to the vibrating sound a rubber band makes when stretched. As the vocal folds are stretched, they become thinner and vibrate more times per second, producing a higher pitch. As the vocal folds are released, they become thicker and vibrate fewer times per second, producing a lower pitch.

The function of the vocal folds is often best improved indirectly, through improved posture, efficient breathing, optimum resonance, freedom and efficiency in the body, and clarity of thought. Focusing directly on the action of the vocal folds can create tensions that disturb their natural function. Consequently, our practical work with the voice here is to learn to feel sound in the whole body. The goal is to view the voice as a full-bodied experience, not merely a localized phenomenon occurring from the neck up. This sensitivity to the feeling of sound in the body helps the speaker make a myriad of subtle, intuitive, semiconscious bodily changes that shape, direct, and focus the tone.

Sound Energy: Charge/Release

Successful sound production depends on energy—structuring and organizing the contrasting sensations of *charge* and *release*. When the breath and body are charging and releasing properly, the way is paved for the fluid production of sound. Experientially, the management of breath and the management of sound are somewhat similar. When working with the breath, we determined that managing the exhalation involved cultivating two distinct physical sensations:

1. Release (the breath falls from the body).
2. Charge (the body carries the breath).

Moving from breath to sound is relatively straightforward: we simply allow sound vibration to ride or to be carried on the outgoing breath:

1. Release (the sound falls from the body). (My concept of the sound falling from the body is deeply indebted to my initial training with master teacher Kristin Linklater and her work revealing the *touch of sound* [Linklater 1976].)
2. Charge (the body carries the sound).

In this manner, the physical sensations of *charge* and *release*—the building up and letting go of energy—in the body and breath make sound production possible. The emphasis shifts from an isolated action of the vocal folds in the throat to a larger integrated action occurring in the whole body.

Exploring on Your Own

Stand upright with your legs about shoulder-width apart. Allow your arms to rest comfortably at your sides. Bend and unbend your knees in a comfortable plié-like action several times. Rest. Repeat this action. Each time your knees bend, allow a very simple, voiced *huh* sound to fall from your body. Each time your knees straighten, receive a new breath. As the breath falls from your body, allow sound vibrations to mix and mingle with the releasing breath. Encourage a clear, nonbreathy release of your voice. Feel the release of physical energy in your whole body. Rest. Now take three steps forward as you sustain an *mmm* sound—a simple hum. Let the sound vibrations mix and mingle with your breath. Feel the buildup of physical energy in the whole body. Repeat several times, remembering to rest briefly in between.

Now let the sound fall from your body during four knee bends and carry the sound while taking four steps forward. Then try five knee bends and five steps forward, followed by six, seven, eight, perhaps more, as many as feel comfortable. Do not push or strain by going beyond what you are able to support. Enjoy the contrasting sensations of sound falling from and being carried by the body— charge and release.

Sound Size: Expand/Contract

Resonance

Resonance is the vehicle for increasing the size and power of the voice. The sound produced by the vocal folds would be weak and difficult to hear without reinforcement and amplification. A resonator is simply a hollow space in which sound waves are in a sense "resounded" as they bounce around like an echo, which increases the power and intensity of the tone. The human voice has three resonators: the oral cavity, the pharynx, and the nasal cavity—the hollow spaces in the mouth, throat, and nose respectively (see Figure 7.1).

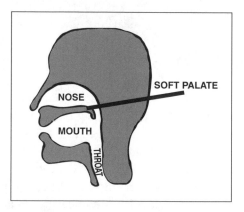

Figure 7.1 Resonating Spaces

The impulse to speak is accompanied by a natural expansion of the resonators. The greater the mental and emotional need, the greater the degree of expansion. After the desire to communicate is exhausted, the expanded resonators naturally and reflexively recoil or contract, marking a return to ease and equilibrium until a new impulse to communicate sets the resonators in motion again. A change in a resonator's size is directly linked to a change in its shape. When you open and close your mouth, for example, you not only increase and decrease the size of the oral cavity, you modify its shape as well.

The size and shape of the vocal resonators determine the voice's quality and color. Labels such as warm, strident, heavy, shrill, shallow, hollow, bright, nasal, light, trapped, pleasant (and a host of others, both complimentary and derogatory) usually refer to qualities of resonance created by the size and shape of the resonating spaces. These adjustments in size and shape occur primarily in the mouth and the throat, not in the nose. The mouth and throat are quite flexible—the lips, jaw, tongue, soft palate, throat, even the cheeks, are constantly expanding and contracting to serve the expressive needs of the speaker.

Although the nasal resonator makes an important contribution to vocal resonance, you can't adjust its size or shape directly, because its walls are made primarily of bone and cartilage and are essentially inflexible. The degree of nasal resonance present in the voice is determined largely by the action of the soft palate—the flexible, fleshy rear portion of the roof of the mouth—which functions somewhat like a floodgate. When lowered it diverts sound vibrations into the nasal resonator; when elevated it diverts sound vibrations into the mouth (see Figure 7.1). Consequently, our practical work on resonance focuses exclusively on making adjustments in the size and shape of the mouth and throat.

The resonance created in the mouth and throat is not unlike the treble and bass speakers of a stereo system. The pocket of resonant energy created in the mouth (the upper resonating space) is the *tweeter*; the pocket of resonant energy created in the throat (the lower resonating space) is the *woofer*. The upper resonating space (the mouth) provides the voice with light, bright, brilliant, ringing vocal resonance. The lower resonating space (the throat) provides the voice with heavy, dark, rich, deep vocal resonance.

Vocal resonance is balanced when more or less equal emphasis is given to both the upper and lower resonating spaces. It is as if the stereo speaker dial is centered midway between treble and bass: the upper resonating space (the mouth) gives the sound clarity and brilliance, while the lower resonating space (the throat) gives the sound weight, depth, and carrying power. A voice with too much mouth resonance is thin, light, and shrill. A voice with too much throat resonance can be heavy, muffled, and unintelligible. A balanced tone, however, simultaneously produces a brilliant and warm sound that is easily understood and has sufficient carrying power.

This doesn't mean that all acts of expression require balanced resonance. Nevertheless, a balanced tone provides the most opportunity for varied and flexible expression. Unbalanced voices tend to be arrested and fixed and are capable of little variation or modification in quality and color. A speaker with a balanced tone can shift easily between light, bright tones and dark, heavy tones and all the many variations in between. It's like mixing water and earth. The result is a type of clay or mud with varying consistencies and textures. The more water, the thinner the clay (the brighter and lighter the sound). The more earth, the thicker the clay (the darker and heavier the sound). The combinations are infinite, from a slippery soup to squishy mud to thick, rich mortar. The possibilities are as diverse and as variable as the thoughts and feelings of the speaker (Alderson 1979).

Tuning the Vowel Space

Practical work on balancing the resonance of the voice involves adjusting the size and shape of the upper and lower resonating spaces so that vowel sounds can receive their optimum resonance. This process is called *tuning the vowel space*. The vowel space is a by-product of a pocket of resonant energy created in the mouth and a pocket of resonant energy created in the throat. When the right vowel space is created, the right vowel sound emerges. Vowel sounds are often thought of as a series of movements made by the lips, jaw, and tongue. While this is correct as far as it goes, a vowel sound is not created so much by the movement of the articulators but by the hollow space that their movement creates in the mouth and throat. The process of adjusting the vowel space for improved resonance is a complex science involving *harmonics, overtones, frequencies, partials,* and *formats* (McKinney 1994) that is beyond the scope of this book. However, practical work on tuning the vowel space is relatively simple to explain: some previously dormant muscles must be activated to enhance resonance, while other tense muscles inhibiting resonance must be released. It is both an *active* and a *passive* process.

When you tune a vowel, all moveable parts of the mouth and throat are "wiggled" into proper alignment until you find a sweet spot—the point at which maximum vibration is produced with minimal effort. It's like tuning in a radio: you keep moving the dial around until you find the spot where you receive the best reception. It involves the readjustment of the size and shape of the entire vocal tract: not so much pronounced muscular movements but subtle shifts in the moveable parts of the mouth and throat that affect the manner in which the vowel sound vibrates in the body. In fact, the vowel is often tuned so imperceptibly that it can be difficult to know precisely how the mouth and throat were adjusted for increased power and purer quality. In the majority of cases, tuning the vowel space involves expanding the size of the resonator, providing room for a fuller, more vibrant tone. Just as a concert grand piano has more power than a baby grand, the larger the resonating spaces, the more powerful and full the voice. Vowel tuning is enhanced by:

1. An increased awareness of vibration—the feeling of the vowel sound resonating in the body.
2. Flexibility and fluidity in the moveable parts of the mouth and throat.
3. A sense of ease and expansiveness in the upper and lower resonating spaces.

Forward/Open/Full Vowels
A practical method of tuning the vowel space involves training the resonator to expand and contract in all directions by vocalizing on the *ee, ah, oo* vowels (as in the words *me, ma, moo*, respectively). When progressing through this three-vowel sequence—a type of articulatory triangle—all the moveable parts of the mouth receive a complete articulatory workout (see Figure 7.2). All other vowel sounds fall somewhere in between the "extreme" tongue, jaw, and lip positions needed to make these three vowel sounds. The tongue arch moves from its most forward position, on *ee*, to its most back position, on *oo*. The jaw moves from its most narrow opening, on *ee*, to its widest opening, on *ah*. The lips move from their most rounded position, on *oo*, to their most relaxed position, on *ah*, and to a slightly smiling position, *ee*. A fluid and seamless transition from *ee* to *ah* to *oo* requires a flexible, stable, well-tuned resonator. Most important, the resonance of a vowel

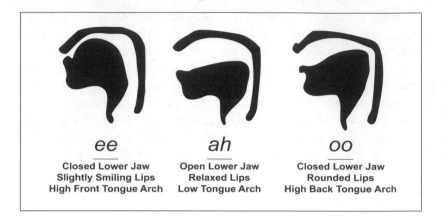

ee
Closed Lower Jaw
Slightly Smiling Lips
High Front Tongue Arch

ah
Open Lower Jaw
Relaxed Lips
Low Tongue Arch

oo
Closed Lower Jaw
Rounded Lips
High Back Tongue Arch

Figure 7.2 Vowel Space

is said to be balanced when it has the qualities characteristic of the forward *ee* vowel, the open *ah* vowel, and the full *oo* vowel:

1. A *forward* tone falls freely into the front of the mouth. Its vibration can be sensed directly on the lips, teeth, and hard palate. A forward tone has a bright, light, ringing quality that gives the voice clarity and vibrancy. It occurs when the upper resonating space (the mouth) is making an optimum contribution to the tone. A forward tone can be sensed most fully on the *ee* vowel. The forward tongue position and narrow jaw opening of the *ee* vowel directs the sound into the very front of the mouth and produces a solid vibration in the upper resonating space. Optimum resonance in the upper resonating space is accompanied by the feeling of vibration in the head and face, or *mask*. It occurs when sympathetic sound vibrations resounding in the mouth travel upward through the bones of the head and face.

2. An *open* tone is characterized by expansiveness, freedom, and fluidity in both the upper and lower resonating spaces. An open tone travels freely through the throat and mouth without constriction or interference. This feeling of openness integrates the upper and lower resonating spaces and is essential to balanced resonance. An open tone can be sensed most fully on the *ah* vowel. The wide jaw position and relatively low tongue position of the *ah* vowel ensure the vocal vibrations are traveling freely through both the upper and lower resonating spaces.

3. A *full* tone is characterized by depth, weight, and solidity. It has a dark, warm, sonorous quality that provides power and substance. It occurs when the lower resonating space makes an optimal contribution to the tone. A full tone can be sensed most completely on the *oo* vowel. The high back tongue position and rounded lips of the *oo* vowel allow optimal vibration in the lower resonating space. Optimum resonance in the lower resonating space is accompanied by the feeling of vibrations resounding in the chest. This occurs when sympathetic sound vibrations in the throat travel downward through the bones of the chest.

When the actor is working for balanced resonance, a forward, open, full tone should be cultivated on all vowel sounds. Every vowel should have resonant properties characteristic of the forward *ee*, the open *ah*, and the full *oo* sounds. When these three vowels are well-tuned, all others tend to fall into place.

Exploring on Your Own

Select any comfortable pitch in the middle of your vocal range, not too high and not too low. Sustain an *ee* vowel for several seconds but not longer than you are able to support the sound. Direct the vibration forward into the front of your mouth. Make any necessary adjustments in the vowel space to produce a vibrant forward tone. Sense the vibrations directly on your lips, teeth, and hard palate. Let the vibrations play freely in your head and face. Rest and repeat.

Next, sustain an *ah* vowel on the same pitch for several seconds but not longer than you are able to support the sound. Encourage a sense of openness and expansiveness in your mouth and throat. The *ah* vowel should travel freely and fluidly through the resonating spaces. Make any necessary adjustments in the vowel space to produce a free and open tone. Rest and repeat.

Now sustain an *oo* vowel for several seconds but not longer than you are able to support the sound. Enjoy the warmth, weight, depth, and richness of this vowel sound. Make any necessary adjustments in the vowel space to produce a rich and full tone. Let the vibrations play freely in your chest cavity. Rest and repeat.

Now progress through this three-vowel sequence, from the forward *ee* to the open *ah* to the full *oo*, on one sustained tone. As you move from vowel to vowel, you should experience a great deal of expanse and freedom in the upper and lower resonating spaces. Notice the point at which each vowel sound takes on its richest resonance. When the upper and lower resonating spaces are adequately expanded, it is possible to sequence from vowel to vowel without any abrupt shift or deterioration in tone. All three vowels possess an equally rich and stable resonance that is best described as forward, open, and full. Repeat this three-vowel sequence several times using a variety of comfortable pitches.

Repeat the above exploration while closing off your nostrils with your thumb and index finger. When you produce the *ee*, *ah*, and *oo* vowels, you should not experience any ringing or buzzing in your nose. (In English, the nasal resonator is only used directly when making the *m*, *n*, and *ng* consonants.) If sound vibrations are ringing in your nose, the soft palate is not adequately expanded and sound vibrations are being inappropriately shifted into the nasal resonator. If this occurs, encourage a great sense of openness and expansiveness in the back of the mouth and throat. Wiggle all the moveable parts of your mouth around until you feel the sound vibrations leave your nose and fall forward into your mouth.

Sound Progression: Center/Periphery

Progression refers to the degree of fluidity and ease with which the speaker can progress or travel up and down the vocal range. The middle voice, the largest area, comprises those pitches in and around the center of the vocal range. The pitches of the upper and lower voice lie on the periphery, above and below the middle voice. The average vocal range is approximately two octaves (fifteen white keys on the piano keyboard). While some voices may extend further, a two-octave range is more than adequate for fluid expression.

The upper, middle, and lower voice comprises a series of consecutive pitches that share a similar and consistent quality and color. Like the notes on the piano keyboard, the higher vocal pitches have a light and bright quality, the lower vocal pitches have a warm and dark quality. The middle vocal pitches reflect a balance of light and dark, bright and warm qualities, and are the most dynamic and flexible. Most speech occurs in the middle voice, with the upper and lower voice used to express the most extreme and powerful thoughts and feelings. As the ability to progress up and down the musical scale is improved, the whole voice is developed and strengthened. Improved range leads to improved resonance, breath control, and tonal quality.

Vocal Center

The vocal center falls midway between the highest and lowest notes of the speaker's range. It is the very center of the middle voice. The bulk of the actor's work, like daily conversation, falls in and around the vocal center, but one should always sense the notes above and below and the possibilities they offer.

Many speakers pitch their vocal center above or below what is normal and healthy for their voices. Voices pitched too high have limited room to travel upward. Voices pitched too low have limited room to travel downward. Only when the vocal center is clearly established can the full range be accessed with ease and spontaneity. The vocal center is not a position to be maintained but a place the voice consistently moves through and returns to as it progresses up and down the musical scale. The journey of a free and flexible voice begins in the center, travels to the periphery, and returns again to the center before taking another voyage to the periphery. The vocal center is a balanced point of efficient departure.

It is common for the vocal center to shift in the course of developing and strengthening the range. As new pitches are gained in the upper and lower voice, the vocal center readjusts to accommodate the increased range. Additionally, some days we experience our vocal center a little higher, other days a little lower. The vocal center is more flexible than commonly thought and reflects the varying degrees of tenseness and laxness in the whole body. Tired and lethargic bodies center lower, just as active and alert bodies center higher. Allowing the vocal center to shift when necessary reflects a profound kind of sensory awareness of the changing and flexible nature of the human person. It is essential to being yourself.

Periphery

Progression through the upper and lower voice is aided by a series of shifting physical sensations that occur naturally in the body. Certain physical sensations are particularly suited to exploring the upper voice, and certain physical sensations are particularly suited to exploring the lower voice. These contrasting physical sensations help us express our feelings. For reasons not completely understood, certain thoughts and feelings find their expressive life in the upper voice, while others find their expressive life in the lower voice. Just as the high notes on the piano keyboard have a light, bright, energetic emotive quality and the lower notes on the piano keyboard have a heavy, dark, languid emotive quality, the human voice has a similar organization and structure. Consequently, cultivating specific physical sensations corresponding to these emotive qualities makes expanding one's vocal range not merely a technical exercise but an organic and psychological exploration as well. In the fluid and integrated expression of thought and feeling, shifts in vocal range are ideally accompanied by corresponding shifts in sensations in the whole body.

1. *Energy: Charge/Release.* To access the upper and lower voice, we need to regulate our physical energy. As we move up the musical scale, more energy is required; as we move down the musical scale, less energy is required. Ideally, this increase of energy is experienced not simply in the voice but in the entire body. A limp and lifeless body does not have the necessary energy to access the upper voice. Similarly, a radiant and racing body does not have the necessary release to access the lower voice. Focusing on reorganizing the energy of the body is more useful than reaching for high notes and pushing for low notes.

2. *Size: Expand/Contract.* Ideally, movement in the upper and lower voice is accompanied by gradual increases in the size of the resonators. As the pitch moves progressively up or down the musical scale away from the vocal center, the size of the resonators gradually needs to increase. Pitches in the upper and lower voice require more resonant space than pitches in the middle voice. This increased expansion frees the tone and prohibits the tightening, pressing, and squeezing that occur when an individual reaches for high notes or presses for low notes.

3. *Speed: Fast/Slow.* To access the upper and lower voice, we need to regulate the speed with which our vocal folds vibrate—faster when moving up the musical scale and slower when moving down the musical scale. While the benefits of focusing on the seemingly autonomous action of the vocal folds is questionable, thoughts and feelings associated with the upper voice are most often sensed in the body as fast, while thoughts and feelings associated with the lower voice are most often sensed in the body as slow. Substitut-

ing fast and slow for the traditional descriptions of high and low tends to prevent reaching up for high notes and pressing down for low notes.

4. *Weight: Heavy/Light.* To access the upper and lower voice, we need to regulate the weight of the sound. Allowing the body to become lighter when moving up the scale and heavier when moving down the scale facilitates an integrated exploration of range. In general, the light and bright sounds of the upper voice resonate more fully in the upper resonating space (the mouth) and the warm, full, mellow sounds of the lower voice resonate more fully in the lower resonating space (the throat). Encouraging the free and active interplay of vibrations in the face and head, which are commonly associated with the upper resonating space, and the free and active interplay of vibrations in the chest, which is commonly associated with the lower resonating space, facilitates a fluid and free transition into the upper and lower voice.

The following other physical properties of an expressive action may also be useful when trying to extend our vocal range:

Upper voice: contact, direct, stable, sharp

Lower voice: withdraw, indirect, unstable, diffused

Developing a full vocal range often requires battling biases and stereotypes. These conditioned responses develop for any number of reasons. Many reflect traditional ideas with respect to appropriate masculine and feminine behavior: *That sounds girly. Those sounds are improper for a lady.* Still others are specific and individual, some conscious and others unconscious: *I don't want to sound like my mother. My voice must match my body size.* Sometimes a limited range is the result of being afraid to express oneself. For many actors, work on range is more than strengthening and extending the technical instrument; it means extending and redefining who they are. Extending one's range is ultimately an extension of the whole person. As new pitches in the voice are discovered, new methods of emotional and physical expression are discovered as well. The best approach is to be patient and diligent, simultaneously encouraging both the mind and the body to find new methods of expression.

Exploring on Your Own

Take a moment and find a comfortable starting pitch, somewhere in the middle of your vocal range. Rest. Now send a light and bright *ee* sound (as in *me*) up into your head. This light, bright sound buzzing in your head is the upper voice. Now, drop a deep *oo* sound (as in *moo*) down into your chest. The deep place where this *oo* is rumbling is your lower voice. Once again, find a comfortable pitch in your lower voice. While sustaining the selected pitch, progress through the three-vowel sequence *oo, oh, ah* (as in *moo, mow, ma,* respectively). Rest. Repeat several times. As you repeat the three-vowel sequence, take several steps forward in a released, slow, and heavy manner. Let this released, slow, heavy movement influence the color and quality of your voice. Repeat this three-vowel sequence several times on a number of comfortable pitches in your lower voice. Rest.

Now select a comfortable pitch in your upper voice. While sustaining the selected pitch, progress through the three-vowel sequence *ee, ay, ai* (as in *me, may, my,* respectively). Repeat several times. As you repeat the three-vowel sequence, take several steps forward in a charged, fast, and light manner. Let this charged, fast, light movement influence the quality and color of your voice. Repeat this three-vowel sequence several times on a number of comfortable pitches in your upper voice.

Sound Orientation: Contact/Withdraw

The speech act begins with a period of withdrawal, characterized by an inward and retreating movement, during which the internal thoughts and feelings of the speaker are gathered and assembled. This brief internal period is usually followed by a longer and more sustained period of contact, characterized by a forward and advancing movement, during which these internal thoughts and feelings receive physical form in words, phrases, and sentences and are shared with others. A clear understanding of the content and quality of one's thoughts and feelings and a heartfelt desire to share those thoughts and feelings is essential to effective contact and withdrawal. Either mental and emotional uncertainty or physical timidity can interrupt the fluid and free-flowing inward and outward orientation of the speaker. Efficient and coordinated vocal production is linked directly to the successful sequencing of contact and withdrawal.

Sound Flow: Free/Bound

A bound voice is locked or arrested in one place. A free voice is fluid, dynamic, and capable of an infinite variety of adjustments in resonance and range. A free voice is essential to successful expression. Most important, a free voice is able to flow in any direction the thoughts and feelings of the speaker take it.

There are two types of vocal freedom (see Figure 7.3):

1. *Horizontal vocal freedom* is developed by progressing through a full collection of vowel sounds (*ee, ay, ah, oh, oo,* as in *me, may, ma, mow, moo,* for example) on any single pitch in the vocal range. If the speaker can clearly and fluidly move *horizontally* from one vowel to the next without any distortion or interruption in tone, the vowel is said to have been freed *horizontally*.

2. *Vertical vocal freedom* is developed by progressing through a sequence of musical notes on a single vowel sound. *Triads*, *arpeggios*, *five-note scales*, or other melodic musical progressions are used in developing vertical vocal freedom. If the speaker can

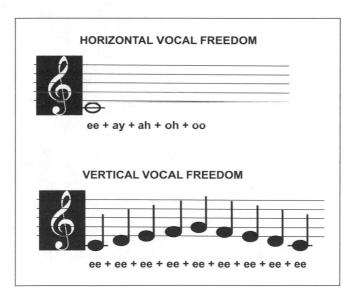

Figure 7.3 Horizontal and Vertical Vocal Freedom

clearly and fluidly move *vertically* from one note to the next without any distortion or interruption in tone, the selected vowel is said to have been freed *vertically*.

The best vocal exercises involve the most possibilities for all the vowel sounds to interact with all the pitches of the vocal range. In this way the voice is strengthened and developed systematically, vowel by vowel and note by note. There are an infinite number of ways to conduct this training and exploration, some of which are presented in Part III, Voice and Body Exercises.

Using the Voice and Body Exercises

These voice and body exercises are divided into four types:

1. Awareness and centering exercises.
2. Lying and breathing exercises.
3. Sitting and sounding exercises.
4. Standing exercises.

A traditional class begins with awareness and centering exercises and progresses sequentially to lying and breathing exercises, sitting and sounding exercises, and finally the standing exercises. In the process, breath and sound are integrated with physical action through a series of sighing, hissing, and sounding actions. In the beginning, it is best to use the exercises in sequence without modification or variation. However, with time and experience, all of the exercises can be modified or adapted for variety and to accommodate different levels of ability.

The exercises labeled *advanced* require a more rigorous exploration of the body, breath, and voice. In general, these exercises should be explored after the fundamental skills have been firmly established. Skip any that are too difficult and return to them later after more skill has been developed.

Certain exercises should be performed at a relatively fast pace, others at a slower pace, because some physical actions are easier than others. With time and experience, all of the exercises can be done at a variety of speeds. In the beginning, the best advice is to go as fast or as slowly as necessary.

Using these exercises successfully depends on properly applying the principles of expressive action and the principles of voice and body presented in the previous chapters. However, the written descriptions of the exercises simply articulate the basic structure or form of the exercise. They don't rearticulate the principles. When learning the exercises, begin by developing an overall understanding of the physical structure of the exercise and then proceed with the important work of applying the principles. Once the essential pattern and structure of the exercise is understood—"roll onto the left side," "toss the arm to the left," "release an *ah* sound"—the principles can be applied—"I *contact* the environment as my body *expands* and *withdraw* as my body *contracts*," "the energy in my body *charges* before it *releases*," "I begin with a centrally initiated weight shift in the pelvis," "my arms are free and integrated with the pelvic center," "my resonance is forward, open, and full."

A superficial understanding of the physical structure of the exercises is relatively easy to obtain. A sophisticated restructuring of the body, breath, and voice requires a diligent and conscientious application of the principles. All the exercises are designed to reflect the physical structure of the major properties of an expressive action. All the exercises, in one form or another, charge and release, expand and contact, contract and withdraw, as the whole body moves from the center to the periphery in a free-flowing manner. An awareness of this structure is essential to integrated and successful practice.

The exercises are built around the following:

Integrated weight shifts.
The center of movement—the pelvis.
Upper body sequence (pelvis + rib cage + head).
Lower body sequence (pelvis + knee + foot).
Creasing and decreasing thigh socket.
Breath management.
The center of breathing—the diaphragm.
Falling/carrying the breath.
Falling/carrying the sound.

Upper and lower breathing spaces.
Upper and lower resonating spaces.
Balanced resonance.
Tuning the vowel space.
Forward, open, and full tone.
Range.
Vocal center.
Upper, middle, and lower voice.
Horizontal vocal freedom.
Vertical vocal freedom.

Awareness and Centering Exercises

Feeling/Thinking/Doing

This exercise is designed to put you in touch with your immediate physical, mental, and emotional experience and to increase your awareness of the manner in which thoughts, feelings, and physical sensation are interconnected.

Step 1: Rest
Lie on your back with your legs comfortably lengthened and your arms resting comfortably at your sides. Your legs and feet will rotate naturally and fall outward toward the floor. Take a luxuriating yawn and full-bodied stretch. Rest.

Step 2: Physical State
Imagine that your body is (select one) *heavy, itching, tingling, light, racing, warm, cold, burning, swelling, numb, pulsating, pressured, tight, jerky, twitching, hurt, restless, resting, sore.* How does this physical state affect your thinking? How does this physical state make you feel?

Step 3: Mental State
Imagine that your mind is (select one) *alert, wandering, judging, cloudy, confused, rational, planning, worrying, calculating, irrational, composed, frustrated, pondering, introspective, inattentive, peaceful.* How

does this mental state affect your body? How does this mental state make you feel?

Step 4: Emotional State

Imagine that you are feeling (select one) *happy, sad, giddy, angry, joyful, hopeful, fearful, depressed, loving, disgusted, rage, lonely, hurt, aloof, difficult, content, greedy, giving, bratty.* How does this emotional state affect your body? How does this emotional state affect your thinking?

Step 5: Repetition

Repeat several more times, selecting different physical, mental, and emotional states to explore. Focus on the interconnectedness of your body, mind, and emotions.

Giving and Receiving

This exercise is designed to put you in touch with your natural breathing rhythm. The rhythm of the breath is relatively simple: the breath comes, the breath goes, there is a slight pause, a new breath comes and goes, as the pattern repeats. The rhythm of the breath is often compared to the rise and fall of ocean waves. Each breath, like each wave of the ocean, is punctuated with a clearly defined beginning, middle, and end. Whether the quality of your breathing is calm and serene or rough and tumultuous, whether you are at rest or at play, whether you are expressing complex thoughts or insignificant banter, deep feelings or ambivalent retorts, long sentences or short phrases, whispering or shouting—the essential rhythm of your breath is consistent and universal. There is always an inhalation followed by an exhalation. Cultivating the ability to monitor the rhythm of your breath without inhibiting its involuntary flow is an essential first step in learning to organize the physical life of the breath in your body.

Thinking of breathing in the context of *receiving, giving,* and *resting* promotes a free, effortless, rhythmic approach to managing your incoming and outgoing breath. Central to the idea of giving and receiving is recognizing that the acts of inhalation and exhalation are inextricably linked. There is not one action of breathing in and another action of breathing out but rather one integrated breathing action experienced in two phases. Inhalation and exhalation share a reciprocal and corresponding *giving* and *receiving* relationship. It is impossible to experience one without the other.

Step 1: Giving and Receiving

Lie on your back. Allow your knees to bend so that the soles of your feet are making solid contact with the floor. Your feet should be about shoulder-width apart and as close to your pelvis as possible without causing strain or discomfort. Don't let your knees collapse inward or fall outward. Allow your whole back to lengthen and widen into the floor. Allow your jaw to drop open so that your breath flows freely in and out of your mouth. Become aware of the rising and falling action of your breath. Receive a new breath—inhale. Give your breath away—exhale. Repeat the cycle. Observe the rhythm of your breath for several moments. Notice how each breath has a clearly defined beginning, middle, and end. Rest and repeat.

Step 2: Major Properties

Observe the giving and receiving action of your breath from five different perspectives—the major properties of an expressive action:

Energy: Charge/Release. Observe the energy of your body increasing and decreasing as your breath enters and leaves your body.

Orientation: Contact/Withdraw. Allow your awareness to travel outward on your outgoing breath and inward on your ingoing breath.

Size: Expand/Contract. Observe how the size of your body increases and decreases to accommodate the incoming and outgoing breath.

Progression: Center/Periphery. Allow the movement of your breath to begin in the center of your body (the middle of your belly) and travel outward to the periphery in all directions (up into your chest and down toward your pelvis).

Free Flow. Allow the breath to come and go without physical or mental interruptions.

Movement Center—Simple Weight Shifting

This exercise is designed to put you in touch with the movement center—the pelvis.

Basic Exercise

Lie on your back with your legs and arms lengthened. Your feet should be comfortably close together, your arms resting away from the body at approximately a forty-five-degree angle. The legs and feet will rotate naturally and fall outward toward the floor. Slowly and fluidly shift the weight of your pelvis to the left and then to the right side. Repeat this shifting action several times (see Figure 9.1) in a continuous and uninterrupted manner. Rest.

The swinging action of the pelvis is similar to a pendulum swinging gently and easily from side to side. As you shift your pelvis to the right side, notice how your left leg and foot are drawn inward toward your pelvis as your leg and foot on the right side of your body are extended downward away from your pelvis. As you shift your pelvis to the left side, notice how your right leg and foot are drawn inward toward your pelvis as your leg and foot on the left side of your body are extended downward away from your pelvis.

Relieve any muscular tension that is preventing your legs from responding to the movement of your pelvis. Repeat this swinging movement for several moments. Luxuriate in this centered weight shift in your pelvis. Rest. Repeat as necessary.

Breathing Center—Panting

This exercise is designed to put you in touch with the breathing center—the diaphragm.

Basic Exercise

Lie on your back. Allow your knees to bend so that the soles of your feet are making solid contact with the floor. Your feet should be about

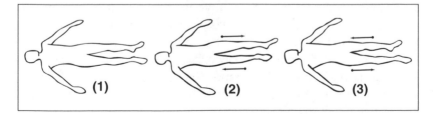

Figure 9.1 Simple Weight Shift

shoulder-width apart and as close to your pelvis as possible without causing strain or discomfort. Don't let the knees collapse inward or fall outward. Allow your whole back to lengthen and widen into the floor. Initiate a quick and vibrant panting action from the diaphragm. Allow the panting action to escalate in intensity. When the panting action has run its course, allow it to subside and resolve easily and naturally. The panting action should have a clearly defined beginning, middle, and end. Keep the panting sequence relatively short. Enjoy the deep sensation of activity and vitality produced in your whole body by the action of your breath. Repeat this process two or three more times. Rest in between as necessary. Take care not to hyperventilate.

Rocking Exercise I

Rocking exercises are a simple method of coordinating the centered movement of your breath with the centered movement of your body. Your focus is simultaneously on your movement center and your breathing center. The purpose is to encourage your movement center (your pelvis) to work in harmony with your breathing center (your diaphragm). These relatively small rocking movements of your breath and body will ultimately pave the way for the integration of larger and more physically demanding movements of your breath and body.

Step 1: Basic Exercise

Lie on your back. Allow your knees to bend and make a deep crease in your thigh socket, folding your legs in and upward toward your chest. As the legs fold into the chest, gently grasp the knees with your hands. Allow your whole spine to lengthen and widen into the floor. You should not feel as if you are holding your legs in the air but rather that they are stabilized and supported from the pelvis. Encourage the sensation of your legs floating or hovering above your pelvis. Initiate a gentle rocking action in your pelvis by creasing and de-creasing your thigh sockets. This creasing and de-creasing action will move your bent knees inward toward your chest and then outward away from your chest. Make this repetitive movement quite small and rhythmical. Your arms do not need to assist in this gentle rocking action. Encourage freedom and flexibility in your thigh sockets. Allow this centered movement to radiate through your whole body. Relieve any unnecessary muscular tension that is keeping the energy of your body from flowing freely from the center to the periphery. Rest. Repeat this gentle rocking action until your lumbar spine and thigh sockets feel loose and limber and your whole body is rocking on the floor in response to the action of your pelvis.

Step 2: Adding the Breath

Continue the gentle rocking action. Drop your jaw. Allow your breath to enter and leave the body in concert with the rocking action of your pelvis. Do not pump your breath. Simply allow your breath to come and go in concert with the rocking action in your pelvis. Integration has been achieved when the movement of your breath and the movement of your body seem inseparable—when your body and breath *charge* and *release* in harmony with one another. Play with varying the speed of the rocking action. Rest. Repeat.

Rocking Exercise 2

In this exercise the relationship of your legs and feet is reconfigured.

Step 1: Basic Exercise

Lie on your back. Allow your knees to bend so that the soles of your feet are making solid contact with the floor. Your feet should be about shoulder-width apart and as close to your pelvis as possible without causing strain or discomfort. Don't let your knees collapse inward or rotate outward. Allow your whole back to lengthen and widen into the floor. Initiate a gentle rocking action in your pelvis and lumbar spine by gently creasing and de-creasing your thigh sockets. As you crease and de-crease your thigh sockets, your pelvis and lumbar spine will gently arch up away from the floor and then round back down into the floor. Make this repetitive movement quite small and rhythmical. Encourage freedom and flexibility in your thigh sockets. Let this centered movement radiate through your whole body. Relieve any unnecessary muscular tension that is keeping the energy in your body from flowing freely from the center to the periphery. Rest. Repeat this gentle rocking action until your lumbar spine and thigh sockets feel loose and limber.

Step 2: Adding the Breath

Same as for Rocking Exercise 1.

Lying and Breathing Exercises

These lying and breathing exercises are integrated explorations of the breath and the body. Typically, during these lying exercises, your legs are tossed and swung and raised and lowered in a variety of positions in a variety of patterns. The purpose of these exercises is to develop the ability to move your pelvis, legs, and feet in a substantial way without interfering with the action of your breath. When this skill is mastered, it is possible to stand upright and make bold and momentous physical movements without disrupting the flow of the breath.

The following general directives apply to all the exercises in this section:

- The movement of your legs and feet should begin with a weight shift in your pelvis.
- The movement of your legs and feet is initiated and regulated by creasing and de-creasing your thigh sockets. (This is similar to folding and unfolding a sheet of paper. When a piece of paper is folded in half, a crease is formed in the center. Similarly, when your legs are lifted up and away from the floor, a crease or fold is created in your thigh sockets. Creasing the thigh sockets lifts your legs and feet up and away from the floor. De-creasing your thigh sockets lowers your legs and feet downward toward the floor.)

■ The swinging and tossing action of your legs moves from the center to the periphery—beginning in your pelvis through your knee through your ankle to your foot.

■ When you are lying on the floor and moving your legs and feet, your upper body is not tense and tight, nor is it collapsed and relaxed; it is active and alive, stabilizing and grounding your body as your legs are tossed or swung and raised or lowered.

Phrasing

A well-coordinated physical phrase promotes fluid and integrated breathing. As you explore the lying and breathing exercises, observe the structured rhythm of the physical phrase. Allow each physical phrase to have a clearly defined beginning, middle, and end. To help you coordinate the physical phrase, each phrase is assigned a specific number of counts. An exercise with four phrases and eight counts in each phrase is a 4–8 count phrase. The first number is the number of times the phrase is repeated. The second number is the number of counts in each phrase. A 4–8 count phrase is typically counted aloud as 1-2-3-4-5-6-7-8, 2-2-3-4-5-6-7-8, 3-2-3-4-5-6-7-8, 4-2-3-4-5-6-7-8 (see Figure 10.1).

The counting speed may vary from exercise to exercise. It is best to begin with a comfortable pace that allows the free and fluid movement of the breath and body. With time and experience, the speed can be increased or decreased as needed. Ideally, this structured exploration of the breath and body prepares the way for the well-supported phrasing of language. The various lengths of the counts correspond to the various lengths of phrases and sentences in connected speech. In this manner, the breath is not simply released or sustained, but rather initiates, develops, and resolves in much the same way that a sentence has a clearly defined beginning, middle, and end.

1ST PHRASE	R E S T	2ND PHRASE	R E S T	3RD PHRASE	R E S T	4TH PHRASE	R E S T
1-2-3-4-5-6-7-8		2-2-3-4-5-6-7-8		3-2-3-4-5-6-7-8		4-2-3-4-5-6-7-8	

Figure 10.1 Phrasing

Four Steps

A typical lying and breathing exercise progresses through four steps:

Step 1. *Basic exercise:* exploring the physical form of the exercise
Step 2. *Phrasing:* counting the exercise in time
Step 3. *Release—breath falls from the body:* exploring the exercise while *sighing* on a voiceless *huh* sound
Step 4. *Charge—body carries the breath:* exploring the exercise while *hissing* on an uninterrupted, voiceless *sss* sound

When describing an exercise in writing, it is often difficult to communicate precisely where a new breath is taken and precisely where the breath is let go. The question of when to inhale and when to exhale is complicated and can only be explained in general terms. With time and experience, the breath is released, sustained, and replaced organically and ineffably in concert with the movement of the body. Integrated breathing and moving is a natural and normal human activity. When it feels right, it probably is right.

Pelvic Tilt

See Figures 10.2 and 10.3.

Step 1: Basic Exercise

1. Lie on your back. Allow your knees to bend so that the soles of your feet are making solid contact with the floor. Your feet should be about shoulder-width apart and as close to your pelvis as possible without causing strain or discomfort. Don't let your knees collapse inward or fall outward. Allow your whole back to lengthen and widen into the floor.

2. In an easy and fluid movement, slowly tilt your pelvis in an upward direction approximately two inches off the floor.

3. Reverse the tilting action so that your pelvis returns to the floor.

Observe the creasing and de-creasing action in your thigh sockets, which tilts your pelvis in an upward and downward direction. Repeat four times. Rest.

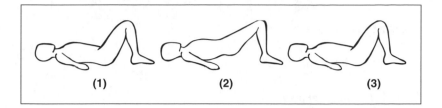

Figure 10.2 Basic Exercise: Pelvic Tilt

Step 2: Phrasing
Repeat the pelvic tilt exercise, counting aloud in four phrases with two counts in each phrase—*1-2, 2-2, 3-2, 4-2*. Tilt your pelvis up on the first count and down on the second count of each phrase. Take a brief rest after completing the fourth two-count phrase.

Step 3: Release—Breath Falls from the Body
Repeat the pelvic tilt exercise. Receive a new breath each time your pelvis tilts upward. Allow your breath to fall from your body on a simple *sigh*—a voiceless *huh* sound—each time your pelvis tilts downward and returns to the floor. The sensation of your body yielding to gravity should accompany the passive release of your outgoing breath.

Step 4: Charge—Body Carries the Breath
Repeat the pelvic tilt exercise. Receive a new breath at the top of the first phrase just as your pelvis tilts upward. Immediately after receiving the breath, allow your body to carry the breath on a simple *hiss*— an uninterrupted voiceless *sss* sound—over the entire *4-2* count phrase. The sensation of your body carrying your breath should accompany the actively sustained *sss* sound.

	1ST PHRASE		2ND PHRASE		3RD PHRASE		4TH PHRASE		
STEP 1	TILT UP	TILT DOWN	TILT UP	TILT DOWN	TILT UP	TILT DOWN	TILT UP	TILT DOWN	R
STEP 2	1	- 2	2	- 2	3	- 2	4	- 2	E
STEP 3	*	SIGH	*	SIGH	*	SIGH	*	SIGH	S
STEP 4	* SSSSSSSSSSSSSSSSSSSSSSSSSSSSSSSSSSSSSSSSSSSSSSSSSSSSSSSSSSSSSSSSSSSSSSSSSSSS								T

* = receive a new breath
ssss = a sustained "s" sound

Figure 10.3 Pelvic Tilt

Partial Bridge

See Figures 10.4 and 10.5.

Step 1: Basic Exercise

1. Lie on your back. Allow your knees to bend so that the soles of your feet are making solid contact with the floor. Your feet should be about shoulder-width apart and as close to your pelvis as possible without causing strain or discomfort. Don't let your knees collapse inward or fall outward. Allow your whole back to lengthen and widen into the floor.

2. In an easy and fluid movement, slowly roll your pelvis in an upward direction away from the floor (the same *tilting action* performed in the previous exercise). Then continue rolling your pelvis upward until the weight of your body is balanced evenly over your shoulders and your feet. Allow your spine and legs to follow your rising pelvis. This will cause your belly to float upward toward the ceiling. Your shoulder girdle and head should remain in contact with the floor. The muscles of your upper legs and buttocks remain soft and free throughout the movement. Your legs remain stable and aligned. The soles of your feet are well grounded, lengthening and widening into the floor. Avoid muscling your body upward by lifting in your chest or pushing in your legs and feet.

3. Reverse the rolling action, lowering your spine toward the floor one vertebra at a time. Your pelvis returns to the floor last. Observe the de-creasing action in the thigh sockets, which lifts your pelvis up and away from the floor, and the creasing action in the thigh sockets, which lowers your pelvis down toward the floor.

Repeat three times, resting briefly in between each phrase.

Step 2: Phrasing

Repeat the partial bridge exercise, counting aloud in three phrases with eight counts in each phrase—1-2-3-4-5-6-7-8, 2-2-3-4-5-6-7-8, 3-2-3-4-5-6-7-8. Roll your pelvis up on counts 1 through 4 and down on counts 5 through 8. Take a brief rest in between each of the three eight-count phrases.

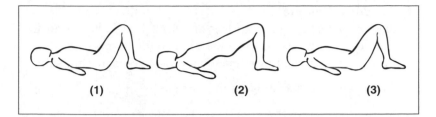

Figure 10.4 Basic Exercise: Partial Bridge

	1st Phrase		R	2nd Phrase		R	3rd Phrase	
Step 1	ROLLING UP	ROLLING DOWN	E	ROLLING UP	ROLLING DOWN	E	ROLLING UP	ROLLING DOWN
Step 2	1 - 2 - 3 - 4 - 5 - 6 - 7 - 8		S	2 - 2 - 3 - 4 - 5 - 6 - 7 - 8		S	3 - 2 - 3 - 4 - 5 - 6 - 7 - 8	
Step 3	*	SIGH	T	*	SIGH	T	*	SIGH
Step 4	* SSSSSSSSSSSSSSSSS			* SSSSSSSSSSSSSSSSS			* SSSSSSSSSSSSSSSSS	

* = receive a new breath
ssss = a sustained "s" sound

Figure 10.5 Partial Bridge

Step 3: Release—Breath Falls from the Body

Repeat the partial bridge exercise. Receive a new breath each time your pelvis rolls up and away from the floor. Allow your breath to fall from your body on a simple *sigh*—a voiceless *huh* sound—each time your pelvis returns to the floor. The sensation of your body yielding to gravity should accompany the passive release of your outgoing breath.

Step 4: Charge—Body Carries the Breath

Repeat the partial bridge exercise. Receive a new breath at the top of each eight-count phrase just as your pelvis tilts upward. Immediately after receiving your breath, allow your body to carry your breath on a simple *hiss*—an uninterrupted voiceless *sss* sound—for the remainder of the eight-count phrase. The sensation of your body carrying the breath should accompany the actively sustained *sss* sound.

Side Roll

See Figures 10.6 and 10.7.

Step 1: Basic Exercise

1. Lie on your back with your legs and arms lengthened. Your feet should be comfortably close together and your arms resting away from your body at approximately a forty-five-degree angle.

2. Draw your left knee upward to your chest.

3. Roll your pelvis over so that you are lying on your right side. As you roll onto your right side, allow your right knee to gently cascade to the floor. Your knee will continue to slide across the floor until your pelvis, torso, and the right side of your face are resting on the floor. Your right arm remains extended out and away from your torso. Allow your left arm to passively follow the movement of your upper body, gently resting across your back at about waist level. (The rolling action should take place in this sequence: pelvis, rib cage, head, and arm.)

4. After a brief pause, reverse the rolling action, so that your body returns to its starting position.

Observe the creasing action in your thigh socket, which draws your leg upward toward your chest, and the de-creasing action in your thigh socket, which assists in rolling over onto your side. Rest. Repeat the side roll on the opposite side.

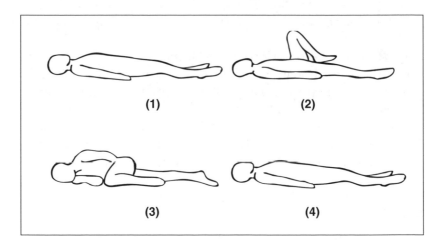

Figure 10.6 Basic Exercise: Side Roll

Step 2: Phrasing

Repeat the side roll exercise. Count the exercise aloud in four phrases with eight counts in each phrase—*1-2-3-4-5-6-7-8, 2-2-3-4-5-6-7-8, 3-2-3-4-5-6-7-8, 4-2-3-4-5-6-7-8*. Roll over onto your right side on the first eight-count phrase and back on the second eight-count phrase. Roll over onto your left side on the third eight-count phrase and back on the fourth eight-count phrase. Take a brief rest between each of the four eight-count phrases.

Step 3: Release—Breath Falls from the Body

Repeat the side roll exercise. Receive a new breath during the first half of each phrase, counts 1 through 4, whenever it's comfortable. Allow your breath to fall from your body on a simple *sigh*—a voiceless *huh* sound—during the second half of each phrase, counts 5 through 8, as your body releases into the floor. The sensation of your body yielding to gravity should accompany the passive release of your outgoing breath.

Step 4: Charge—Body Carries the Breath

Repeat the side roll exercise. Receive a new breath at the top of each eight-count phrase. Immediately after receiving your breath, allow your body to carry your breath on a simple a *hiss*—an uninterrupted voiceless *sss* sound—for the remainder of the eight-count phrase.

Right Side Roll with Breath

	1st Phrase			2nd Phrase	
Step 1	ROLL OVER ONTO THE RIGHT SIDE	R	ROLL BACK ONTO THE LONG-LYING POSITION	R
Step 2	1 - 2 - 3 - 4 - 5 - 6 - 7 - 8	E	2 - 2 - 3 - 4 - 5 - 6 - 7 - 8	E
Step 3	*	SIGH	S	*	SIGH	S
Step 4	* SSSSSSSSSSSSSSSSSSSSSSSSSSSSSS	T	* SSSSSSSSSSSSSSSSSSSSSSSSSSSSSS	T

Left Side Roll

	3rd Phrase			4th Phrase	
Step 1	ROLL OVER ONTO THE LEFT SIDE	R	ROLL BACK ONTO THE LONG-LYING POSITION	R
Step 2	3 - 2 - 3 - 4 - 5 - 6 - 7 - 8	E	4 - 2 - 3 - 4 - 5 - 6 - 7 - 8	E
Step 3	*	SIGH	S	*	SIGH	S
Step 4	* SSSSSSSSSSSSSSSSSSSSSSSSSSSSSS	T	* SSSSSSSSSSSSSSSSSSSSSSSSSSSSSS	T

* = receive a new breath
ssss = a sustained "s" sound

Figure 10.7 Side Roll

Eight Swings

See Figures 10.8 and 10.9.

Step 1: Basic Exercise

1. Lie on your back. Allow your knees to bend and make a deep crease in your thigh sockets. This will fold your legs in and upward toward your chest. Allow your whole back to lengthen and widen into the floor. Extend both arms out and away from the sides of your body at approximately a forty-five-degree angle. You should not feel as if you are holding your legs up in the air but rather that they are stabilized and supported from your pelvis. Encourage the sensation of your legs floating or hovering above your pelvis.

2. With your folded legs centered over your pelvis, initiate a circular swinging action from your pelvis, which will toss your folded legs over to the right side

3. And then back to center.

4. Without interruption, continue the circular swinging action tossing your folded legs over to the left side

5. And then back to center.

These two circles, on the right and left side, unite to form a *figure-eight* pattern. This swinging action is created by an alternating creasing and de-creasing action in your thigh sockets. Allow the momentum created by the swinging action to assist with the movement of your legs. Little or no discernible muscular effort should be sensed in your swinging legs and feet as they are released and supported from your pelvis during the swinging action. Repeat four times. Rest.

Step 2: Phrasing

Repeat the figure-eight swing exercise, counting aloud in four phrases with six counts in each phrase: *1-2-3-4-5-6, 2-2-3-4-5-6, 3-2-3-4-5-6, 4-2-3-4-5-6*. Complete the first figure-eight swing on the first six-count phrase, the second figure-eight swing on the second six-count phrase, and so on. Take a brief rest after completing the fourth six-count phrase.

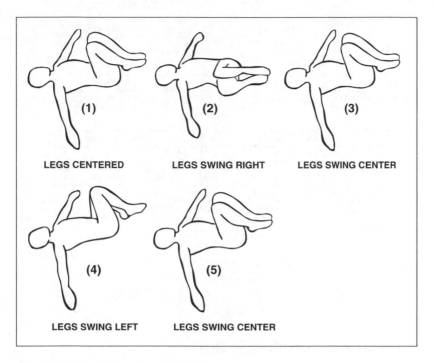

(1) LEGS CENTERED

(2) LEGS SWING RIGHT

(3) LEGS SWING CENTER

(4) LEGS SWING LEFT

(5) LEGS SWING CENTER

Figure 10.8 Basic Exercise: Eight Swings

Step 3: Release—Breath Falls from the Body

Repeat the figure-eight swing exercise. Receive a new breath imme-diately before beginning the first eight swing. Allow your breath to fall from your body on a simple *sigh*—a voiceless *huh* sound—as your legs swing out to the right side. Receive a new breath as your legs swing back through the center of the body. Allow your breath to fall from your body on a simple *sigh*—a voiceless *huh* sound—as your legs swing out to your left side. Continue for the remaining three phrases. The sensation of your body yielding to gravity should accompany the passive release of your outgoing breath.

Step 4: Charge—Body Carries the Breath

Repeat the eight swing exercise. Receive a new breath at the top of each six-count phrase. Immediately after receiving your breath, allow your body to carry your breath on a simple *hiss*—an uninterrupted voice-less *sss* sound—for the remainder of the six-count phrase. The sen-sation of your body carrying the breath should accompany the actively sustained *sss* sound.

	1ST PHRASE				2ND PHRASE			
STEP 1	1 - 2 - 3 - 4 - 5 - 6 - 7 - 8				2 - 2 - 3 - 4 - 5 - 6 - 7 - 8			R
STEP 2	SWING RIGHT	SWING CENTER	SWING LEFT	SWING CENTER	SWING RIGHT	SWING CENTER	SWING LEFT	E
STEP 3	* SIGH	*	SIGH	*	SIGH	*	SIGH	S
STEP 4	* SSSSSSSSSSSSSSSSSSSSSSSSSSSSSSSSSSSSSSSSSSSSSSSSSSSSSSSSSSSSSSSSSSSSSSSSSSS							T

	3RD PHRASE				4TH PHRASE			
STEP 1	3 - 2 - 3 - 4 - 5 - 6 - 7 - 8				4 - 2 - 3 - 4 - 5 - 6 - 7 - 8			R
STEP 2	SWING RIGHT	SWING CENTER	SWING LEFT	SWING CENTER	SWING RIGHT	SWING CENTER	SWING LEFT	E
STEP 3	* SIGH	*	SIGH	*	SIGH	*	SIGH	S
STEP 4	* SSSSSSSSSSSSSSSSSSSSSSSSSSSSSSSSSSSSSSSSSSSSSSSSSSSSSSSSSSSSSSSSSSSSSSSSSSS							T

* = receive a new breath
ssss = a sustained "s" sound

Figure 10.9 Figure-Eight Swings

Alternating Thigh-Socket Creases

See Figures 10.10 and 10.11.

Step 1: Basic Exercise

1. Lie on your back. Allow your knees to bend and make a deep crease in your thigh sockets. This will fold your legs in and upward toward your chest. Allow your whole back to lengthen and widen into the floor. Extend both arms out and away from the sides of your body at approximately a forty-five-degree angle. You should not feel as if you are holding your legs up in the air but rather that they are stabilized and supported from your pelvis. Encourage the sensation of your legs floating or hovering above your pelvis.

2. Shifting your pelvis, move your right and then your left leg and foot in a downward and upward direction toward and away from the floor. During the first alternating sequence, your right and then your left toe tip lightly touch the floor. Repeat two times.

3. During the second alternating sequence, your entire right and left foot touch the floor fluidly—toe, ball, heel—and leave the floor fluidly—heal, ball, toe. Repeat two times.

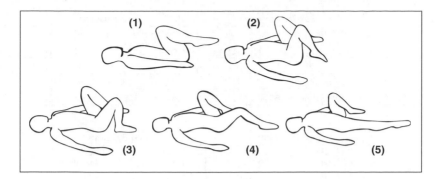

Figure 10.10 Basic Exercise: Alternating Thigh-Socket Creases

4. During the third alternating sequence, your right and then your left foot slide gently across the floor so that each leg is partially lengthened. Repeat two times.

5. During the fourth sequence, your right and then your left foot slide gently across the floor so that each leg is completely lengthened. Repeat two times.

Your legs and feet should remain approximately shoulder-width apart throughout this exercise. Don't let your feet thud and pound into the floor—stabilize their release from your pelvis. Observe the alternating creasing and de-creasing action in your thigh sockets, which raises and lowers your legs and feet toward and away from the floor.

Step 2: Phrasing
Repeat the alternating thigh-socket creases exercise, counting aloud in four phrases with four counts in each phrase—*1-2-3-4, 2-2-3-4, 3-2-3-4, 4-2-3-4*. Allow each toe to touch the floor four times during the first four-count phrase. Allow your whole foot to touch the floor four times during the second four-count phrase. Allow each leg to partially lengthen four times during the third four-count phrase. Allow each leg to completely lengthen four times during the fourth four-count phrase. Take a brief rest after the fourth four-count phrase.

Step 3: Release—Breath Falls from the Body
Repeat the alternating thigh-socket creases exercise. Allow your breath to fall from your body on a simple *sigh*—a voiceless *huh* sound—each

	1ST PHRASE		2ND PHRASE	
Step 1	TOE TIP \ / RIGHT + LEFT	TOE TIP \ / RIGHT + LEFT	WHOLE FOOT \ / RIGHT + LEFT	WHOLE FOOT \ / RIGHT + LEFT
Step 2	1 - 2 - 3 - 4		2 - 2 - 3 - 4	
Step 3	*SIGH *SIGH *SIGH *SIGH		*SIGH *SIGH *SIGH *SIGH	
Step 4	*SSSSSSSSSSSSSSSSSSSSSSSSSSSSSSSS		*SSSSSSSSSSSSSSSSSSSSSSSSSSSSSSSS	

	3RD PHRASE		4TH PHRASE		
Step 1	PARTIAL LEG LENGTHENED \ / RIGHT + LEFT	PARTIAL LEG LENGTHENED \ / RIGHT + LEFT	COMPLETE LEG LENGTHENED \ / RIGHT + LEFT	COMPLETE LEG LENGTHENED \ / RIGHT + LEFT	R E S T
Step 2	3 - 2 - 3 - 4		4 - 2 - 3 - 4		
Step 3	*SIGH *SIGH *SIGH *SIGH		*SIGH *SIGH *SIGH *SIGH		
Step 4	*SSSSSSSSSSSSSSSSSSSSSSSSSSSSSSSS		*SSSSSSSSSSSSSSSSSSSSSSSSSSSSSSSS		

* = receive a new breath
ssss = a sustained "s" sound

Figure 10.11 Thigh-Socket Creases

time your legs release toward the floor. Your breath replaces immediately after exhaling. Take a very quick *catch breath* between each alternating action of your legs and feet. (This breathing action is relatively quick and similar to a pant.) The sensation of your body yielding to gravity should accompany the passive release of your outgoing breath.

Step 4: Charge—Body Carries the Breath

Repeat the alternating thigh-socket creases exercise. Receive a new breath at the top of each four-count phrase. Immediately after receiving your breath, allow your body to carry your breath on a simple *hiss*—an uninterrupted voiceless *sss* sound—over the remainder of the four-count phrase. The sensation of your body carrying your breath should accompany the actively sustained *sss* sound.

Variation

See Figure 10.12.

You can easily modify this exercise by reconfiguring the relationship of your legs and feet: rotate them outward at the thigh socket at approximately a forty-five-degree angle.

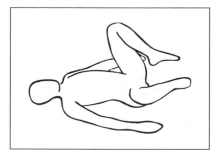

Figure 10.12 Thigh-Socket Creases with Legs in Rotation

Parallel Leg Swings (Advanced)

See Figures 10.13 and 10.14.

Step 1: Basic Exercise

1. Lie on your back with your legs and arms lengthened. Your feet should be comfortably close together and your arms extended away from the body at approximately a forty-five-degree angle.

2. Allow your pelvis to toss or swing your left leg up off the floor. This forward and upward movement of your leg is similar to the action of kicking a football when standing. Let your leg swing as high as is comfortable without bending or locking your knee.

3. When your swinging leg reaches its vertical apex, allow your pelvis to toss it across your right leg in a downward direction. During this swinging action, your knee will bend gently until your left foot lightly touches the floor near the outside of your right knee.

4. After your left foot has touched the floor, initiate a new swinging or tossing action in your pelvis, reversing the process.

5. Your swinging leg returns to its initial lying-down position.

The swinging and tossing of your leg and the bending of your knee should be viewed as one continuous and uninterrupted fluid movement. Observe the creasing action in your thigh socket, which raises your leg up and away from the floor, and the decreasing action in your

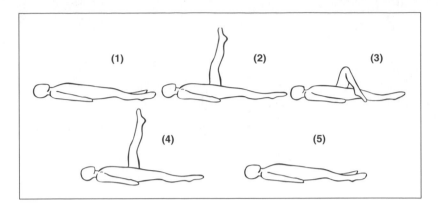

Fiigure 10.13 Basic Exercise: Parallel Leg Swing (Advanced)

thigh socket, which lowers your leg downward toward the floor. Repeat on the opposite side. Repeat two times. Rest.

Step 2: Phrasing
Repeat the parallel leg swing exercise, counting aloud in four phases
with four counts in each phrase—*1-2-3-4, 2-2-3-4, 3-2-3-4, 4-2-3-4.*
Swing your left leg up, over, and back on the first four-count phrase.
Swing your right leg up, over, and back on the second four-count
phrase. Repeat on counts three and four. Take a brief rest after completing the fourth four-count phrase.

Step 3: Release—Breath Falls from the Body
Repeat the parallel leg swing exercise. Receive a new breath each time
your leg swings upward. Allow your breath to fall from your body on
a simple *sigh*—a voiceless *huh* sound—each time your swinging leg
releases toward the floor. The sensation of your body yielding to gravity should accompany the passive release of your outgoing breath.

Step 4: Charge—Body Carries the Breath
Repeat the parallel leg swing exercise. Receive a new breath at the top
of each of the four-count phrases just as your leg begins to swing
upward. Immediately after receiving your breath, allow your body to
carry your breath on a simple *hiss*—an uninterrupted voiceless *sss*
sound—over the remainder of the four-count phrase. The sensation
of your body carrying the breath should accompany the actively sustained *sss* sound.

	1st Phrase		2nd Phrase	
Step 1	SWINGING LEFT LEG UP & OVER	SWINGING LEFT LEG BACK	SWINGING RIGHT LEG UP & OVER	SWINGING RIGHT LEG BACK
Step 2	1 - 2 - 3 - 4		2 - 2 - 3 - 4	
Step 3	* SIGH * SIGH		* SIGH * SIGH	
Step 4	* SSSSSSSSSSSSSSSSSSSSSSSSSSSSSSSS		* SSSSSSSSSSSSSSSSSSSSSSSSSSSSSSSS	

	3rd Phrase		4th Phrase		
Step 1	SWINGING LEFT LEG UP & OVER	SWINGING LEFT LEG BACK	SWINGING RIGHT LEG UP & OVER	SWINGING RIGHT LEG BACK	R
Step 2	3 - 2 - 3 - 4		4 - 2 - 3 - 4		E
Step 3	* SIGH * SIGH		* SIGH * SIGH		S
Step 4	* SSSSSSSSSSSSSSSSSSSSSSSSSSSSSSSS		* SSSSSSSSSSSSSSSSSSSSSSSSSSSSSSSS		T

* = receive a new breath
ssss = a sustained "s" sound

Figure 10.14 Parallel Leg Swing

Leg Swings in Rotation (Advanced)

See Figures 10. 15 and 10.16.

Step 1: Basic Exercise

1. Lie on your back with your legs and arms lengthened. Your feet should be comfortably close together and your arms extended away from your body at approximately a forty-five-degree angle.

2. Allow your pelvis to toss or swing your left leg off the floor away from the center at approximately a forty-five-degree angle. Let your leg swing as high as is comfortable without bending or locking your knee.

3. As your swinging leg reaches its vertical apex, gently allow your knee to bend. Your bent leg is then swung in a downward direction so that the toes of your left foot gently touch the inside of your right knee.

4. After the toes of your left foot have touched your knee, initiate a new tossing or swinging action from your pelvis, reversing the process.

5. Your swinging leg returns to its initial lying-down position.

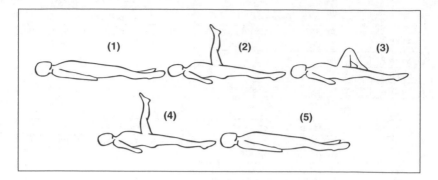

Figure 10.15 Basic Exercise: Leg Swing in Rotation (Advanced)

The swinging and tossing of your leg and the bending of your knee should be viewed as one continuous and uninterrupted fluid movement. Observe the creasing action in your thigh socket, which raises your leg up and away from the floor, and the de-creasing action in your thigh socket, which lowers your leg downward toward the floor. Repeat on your right side. Repeat two times. Rest.

Step 2: Phrasing
Repeat the leg swing in rotation exercise, counting aloud in four phrases with four counts in each phrase—*1*-2-3-4, *2*-2-3-4, *3*-2-3-4, *4*-2-3-4. Swing your right leg up, down, and back on the first four-count phrase. Swing your left leg up, down, and back on the second four-count phrase. Repeat on counts three and four. Take a brief rest after completing the fourth four-count phrase.

Step 3: Release—Breath Falls from the Body
Repeat the leg swing in rotation exercise. Receive a new breath each time your leg swings upward. Allow your breath to fall from your body on a simple *sigh*—a voiceless *huh* sound—each time your swinging leg releases toward the floor. The sensation of your body yielding to gravity should accompany the passive release of your outgoing breath.

Step 4: Charge—Body Carries the Breath
Repeat the leg swing in rotation exercise. Receive a new breath at the top of each of the four-count phrases just as your leg begins to swing upward. Immediately after receiving your breath, allow your body to carry your breath on a simple *hiss*—an uninterrupted voiceless *sss*

	1ST PHRASE		2ND PHRASE	
STEP 1	SWINGING LEFT LEG UP & DOWN	SWINGING LEFT LEG BACK	SWINGING RIGHT LEG UP & DOWN	SWINGING RIGHT LEG BACK
STEP 2	1 - 2 -	3 - 4	2 - 2 -	3 - 4
STEP 3	* SIGH	* SIGH	* SIGH	* SIGH
STEP 4	* SSSSSSSSSSSSSSSSSSSSSSSSSSSSSSSSSSSSS		* SSSSSSSSSSSSSSSSSSSSSSSSSSSSSSSSSSSSS	

	3RD PHRASE		4TH PHRASE		
STEP 1	SWINGING LEFT LEG UP & DOWN	SWINGING LEFT LEG BACK	SWINGING RIGHT LEG UP & DOWN	SWINGING RIGHT LEG BACK	R
STEP 2	3 - 2 -	3 - 4	4 - 2 -	3 - 4	E
STEP 3	* SIGH	* SIGH	* SIGH	* SIGH	S
STEP 4	* SSSSSSSSSSSSSSSSSSSSSSSSSSSSSSSSSSSSS		* SSSSSSSSSSSSSSSSSSSSSSSSSSSSSSSSSSSSS		T

* = receive a new breath
ssss = a sustained "s" sound

Figure 10.16 Leg Swing in Rotation

sound—over the remainder of the four-count phrase. The sensation of your body carrying your breath should accompany the actively sustained sss sound.

Roll-up (Advanced)

See Figures 10.17 and 10.18.

Step 1: Basic Exercise

1. Lie on your back with your legs and arms lengthened. Your feet should be comfortably close together and your arms extended away from your body at approximately a forty-five-degree angle.

2. Tilt your pelvis in a backward and downward direction toward the floor. This will cause your lumbar spine to release into the floor. From this preparatory position, quickly roll your pelvis in a forward and upward direction. This will create a rounding action in your lumbar spine, which moves in sequence through your torso, shoulders, and head.

3. Continue rolling your entire spine forward and up until you arrive in a seated position. In this seated position, your spine is rounded, allowing your torso, head, and shoulders to hover over

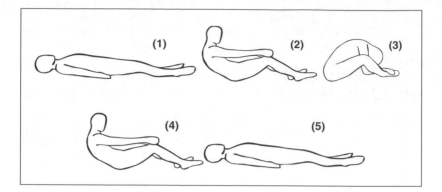

Figure 10.17 Basic Exercise: Roll-up

your legs and feet. (The rolling action of your spine is integrated with corresponding movements in your arms and legs. As your spine rolls upward, your arms and legs are naturally drawn in toward the center of your body. When in the rounded, seated position, your hands rest comfortably near the floor on each foot, and your knees are bent comfortably, with the soles of your feet resting on the floor.

4. Once upright, the rolling action is reversed. Your pelvis tilts in a backward and downward direction and your body unrolls.

5. Your body returns to its initial position.

Observe the creasing and de-creasing action in your thigh sockets, which coordinates the rolling and unrolling action of your spine. Repeat three times. Rest.

It is common to look at the external shape of this exercise and as-sume that what is intended is a simple sit-up. However, when performed correctly, the roll-up is significantly different from the traditional sit-up, in which peripheral abdominal muscles are contracted and often crunched. Here, be sure to direct the rolling-up action from your pel-vis. This allows free and fluid movement of your breath and provides the stability and control necessary to support your lower back.

Step 2: Phrasing

Repeat the roll-up exercise, counting aloud in three phrases with eight counts in each phrase—1-2-3-4-5-6-7-8, 2-2-3-4-5-6-7-8, 3-2-3-4-5-6-7-8. Roll up and down on the first eight-count phrase. Roll up and

	1st Phrase		2nd Phrase		3rd Phrase		
Step 1	ROLLING UP	ROLLING DOWN	ROLLING UP	ROLLING DOWN	ROLLING UP	ROLLING DOWN	R E
Step 2	1 - 2 - 3 - 4 - 5 - 6 - 7 - 8		2 - 2 - 3 - 4 - 5 - 6 - 7 - 8		3 - 2 - 3 - 4 - 5 - 6 - 7 - 8		S
Step 3	* SIGH	* SIGH	* SIGH	* SIGH	* SIGH	* SIGH	T
Step 4	*SSSSSSSSSSSSSSSSSSSS		*SSSSSSSSSSSSSSSSSSSS		*SSSSSSSSSSSSSSSSSSSS		

* = receive a new breath
ssss = a sustained "s" sound

Figure 10.18 Roll-up

down on the second eight-count phrase. Roll up and down on the third eight-count phrase. Take a brief rest after completing the third eight-count phrase.

Step 3: Release—Breath Falls from the Body
Repeat the roll-up exercise. Receive a new breath at the start of each eight-count phrase just as your pelvis initiates the rolling action. Allow your breath to fall from your body on a simple *sigh*—a voiceless *huh* sound—as your upper body yields to gravity and falls over your legs and feet. Receive a new breath when your pelvis reverses its direction and initiates the backward rolling action. Allow your breath to fall from your body on a simple *sigh*—a voiceless *huh* sound—as your upper body releases back down into the floor. The sensation of your body yielding to gravity should accompany the passive release of your outgoing breath.

Step 4: Charge—Body Carries the Breath
Repeat the roll-up exercise. Receive a new breath at the start of each eight-count phrase just as your pelvis initiates the rolling action. Immediately after receiving your breath, allow your body to carry your breath on a *hiss*—an uninterrupted voiceless *sss* sound—over the remainder of the eight-count phrase. The sensation of your body carrying the breath should accompany the actively sustained *sss* sound.

Spine Rounding

See Figures 10.19 and 10.20.

All of the breathing exercises presented have been performed lying down. This is not to suggest that breathing exercises cannot be performed in sitting and standing positions. In fact, almost any sitting or standing exercise can easily be adapted into a breathing exercise. This exercise is one example.

Step 1: Basic Exercise

1. Sit on the floor with your body's weight equally distributed on your pelvis. Allow your lengthened legs to float easily and freely from your thigh sockets and rest comfortably on the floor. Your legs are comfortably close together. Your knees are straight, but not locked, and facing the ceiling. Your pelvis, rib cage, and head are vertical and upright. Your rib cage and head balance evenly and comfortably over your pelvis. Encourage the sensation of your whole torso lengthening and widening.

2. Tilt your pelvis in a downward and backward direction until your whole spine rounds to form a C curve.

3. Once in this rounded position, reverse the action. Tilt your pelvis in a forward and upward direction, which lengthens your spine to its former upright and vertical position.

Observe the creasing and de-creasing action in your thigh sockets, which coordinates the rounding and unrounding action of your spine. Repeat three times.

Step 2: Phrasing

Repeat the spine rounding exercise, counting aloud in three phrases with two counts in each phrase—1-2, 2-2, 3-2. Round your spine on the first count and lengthen your spine on the second count of each phrase. Take a brief rest after completing the third two-count phrase.

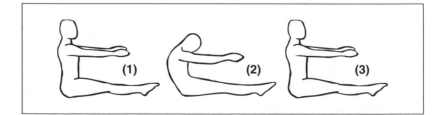

Figure 10.19 Basic Exercise: Spine Rounding

Step 3: Release—Breath Falls from the Body

Repeat the spine rounding exercise. Allow your breath to fall from your body on a simple *sigh*—a voiceless *huh* sound—each time your spine rounds. Receive a new breath each time your spine lengthens. The sensation of your body yielding to gravity should accompany the passive release of your outgoing breath.

Step 4: Charge—Body Carries the Breath

Repeat the spine rounding exercise. Receive a new breath at the top of each phrase just as your pelvis rounds downward. Immediately after receiving your breath, allow your body to carry your breath on a simple *hiss*—an uninterrupted voiceless *sss* sound—over the entire three- or two-count phrase. The sensation of your body carrying the breath should accompany the actively sustained *sss* sound.

Variation

See Figure 10.21.

The spine rounding exercise can be modified by positioning your legs and feet in front of the body in a V—the stride sit position.

	1ST PHRASE		2ND PHRASE		3RD PHRASE		R
STEP 1	ROUND	LENGTHEN	ROUND	LENGTHEN	ROUND	LENGTHEN	E
STEP 2	1	- 2	2	- 2	3	- 2	S
STEP 3	*	SIGH	*	SIGH	*	SIGH	T
STEP 4	* SSSSSSSSSSSSSSSSSSSSSSSSSSSSSSSSSSSSSSSSSSSSSSSSSSSSSSSSSSSSSSSSSSSSSSSSSSSSSSSSSSSSSSS						

* = receive a new breath
ssss = a sustained "s" sound

Figure 10.20 Spine Rounding

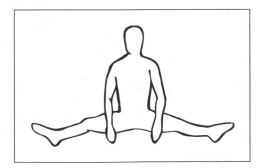

Figure 10.21 Stride-Sit Position

Sitting and Sounding Exercises

These sitting and sounding exercises provide the integrated exploration of the body, breath, and voice. During these exercises, the spine is looped over the legs and feet in a circular pattern (see Figure 11.1) in a variety of sitting positions, on a variety of vowel and consonant sounds, and on a variety of pitches in the vocal range. The purpose of these exercises is to learn to move the upper body in a substantial way without interfering with the action of the breath and voice. When this skill is mastered, it is possible to stand upright and make bold and momentous physical movements in the upper body without disrupting the sound of the voice.

The following general directives apply to all the exercises in this section:

- The looping action begins with a weight shift in the pelvis.
- The looping action is created by creasing and de-creasing the thigh socket. (This is similar to folding and unfolding a sheet of paper. When a piece of paper is folded in half, a crease is formed in the center. Similarly, when the upper body folds over the lower body, a crease is created in the thigh sockets. Creasing the thigh sockets loops the pelvis, rib cage, and head in a downward direction over the legs and feet. De-creasing the thigh sockets loops the

104

pelvis, rib cage, and head in an upward direction away from the legs and feet.)

- Creasing and de-creasing the thigh sockets several times in succession creates a continuous looping action in the upper body. The looping action is performed in a circular pattern and not as an isolated up-and-down movement in which the upper body is systematically raised and lowered over the legs and feet.
- The looping movement occurs in the following sequence: pelvis + rib cage + head.
- Encourage the sensation of the upper body being suspended from the pelvis and hovering outward over the legs and feet rather than collapsing downward toward the floor.
- During this looping action, the arms and legs passively respond to the movement of the body. They should be free and responsive. The legs and feet are not tense and tight but are actively stabilizing and grounding the body.

Four Steps

A typical sitting and sounding exercise progresses through four steps:

Step 1. *Basic exercise:* exploring the physical form of the exercise.
Step 2. *Release—sound falls from the body:* exploring the exercise while sighing on a voiced vowel sound.
Step 3. *Charge—body carries the sound:* exploring the exercise on a sustained vowel or consonant sound.
Step 4. *Working with pitch:* exploring the exercise using a variety of pitches in your vocal range.

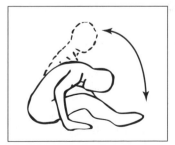

Figure 11.1 Looping

Pitch

In these exercises, the vocal range is often navigated in half steps up and down the musical scale. In certain parts of your range, your voice may be unable to move up and down the scale in half steps. When this happens, simply use any comfortable approximate pitch. As your voice is strengthened and greater control achieved, the half steps will become easier to navigate.

First, the middle voice is explored on a variety of comfortable pitches. Then work proceeds systematically into the lower voice and finally the upper voice. If your voice feels pushed or muscled, return to your middle voice and then begin the journey up or down the scale again.

Phrasing

As you explore these exercises, observe the structured rhythm of the physical and vocal phrases:

- Allow each vocal phrase to have a clearly defined beginning, middle, and end.
- Encourage a stable and steady tone that does not wobble or waiver.
- Avoid excessive tension or wasted breath at either the top or the bottom of the vocal phrase.
- Allow the release of the breath and the onset of sound to occur simultaneously.

Tuning the Vowel

Most of these exercises involve tuning the vowel space (see Chapter 7). This will be enhanced by:

1. Encouraging vibration—the feeling of the sound resonating in the body.
2. Encouraging flexibility and fluidity in the moveable parts of your mouth and throat.
3. Encouraging a sense of ease and expansiveness in the resonating spaces.

Diamond Loop

See Figures 11.2, 11.3, 11.4, and 11.5.

This exercise consists of twelve looping actions, three to the center, three to the right side, three to the left side, and three more to the center.

Step 1: Basic Exercise

1. Begin in a seated position with your body's weight distributed evenly over your pelvis, knees bent, and the soles of your feet touching. The outside edge of each foot rests comfortably on the floor. The space between your legs forms a diamond shape. Your legs rest easily in your thigh socket. The pelvis and spine are vertical and upright. Your rib cage and the head balance evenly and comfortably over your pelvis. Encourage the sensation of your whole torso lengthening and widening.

2. Crease your thigh sockets, looping the pelvis, rib cage, and head in a downward direction over your legs and feet. Then de-crease your thigh sockets, looping the pelvis, rib cage, and head in an

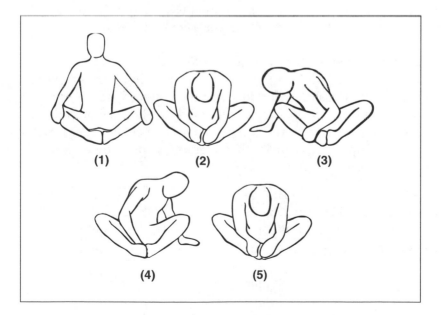

Figure 11.2 Basic Exercise: Looping in Diamond-Sit

upward direction away from your legs and feet. Repeat three times. When finished with the third loop, return to an upright and vertical position.

3. Rotate your pelvis, rib cage, and head to the right. Loop three times over your right leg. Return to an upright and vertical position.

4. Rotate your pelvis, rib cage, and head to the left. Loop three times over your left leg. Return to an upright and vertical position.

5. Rotate your pelvis, rib cage, and head to the center. Loop three times. Rest.

Step 2: Release—Sound Falls from the Body

Repeat the exercise. Receive a new breath at the top of the first phrase as the pelvis initiates the first looping action. Allow a simple *huh* sound to fall from your body each time you loop downward. Receive a new breath each time you loop upward (see Figure 11.3). The sound falling from your body should be in the center of the vocal range—comfortably in your middle voice. (You should sense the possibility of notes above and below your starting pitch.) Allow the looping action of your body to propel the *huh* sound directly into your mouth. The sensation of your body yielding to gravity should accompany the passive release of the voice. Integration has been achieved when the release of your body, breath, and voice seem inseparable.

Step 3: Charge—Body Carries the Sound

Repeat the exercise. Receive a new breath at the top of the first phrase as the pelvis initiates the first looping action. Immediately after receiving the breath, allow a simple *huh* sound to fall from your body. As soon as the *huh* sound arrives in your mouth, catch the sound by closing your lips. The sound is then carried by the body on a simple

		LOOP DOWN	LOOP UP	LOOP DOWN	LOOP UP	LOOP DOWN	LOOP UP
3 LOOPS	CENTER	* HUH	*	HUH	*	HUH	*
3 LOOPS	RIGHT	HUH	*	HUH	*	HUH	*
3 LOOPS	LEFT	HUH	*	HUH	*	HUH	*
3 LOOPS	CENTER	HUH	*	HUH	*	HUH	*

* = receive a new breath

Figure 11.3 Falling onto Sound

hum—an uninterrupted *mmm* sound—for the remainder of the three-loop phrase (see Figure 11.4). The sound should be in the center of the vocal range—comfortably in your middle voice. (You should sense the possibility of notes above and below the starting pitch.) The sensation of your body carrying the sound should accompany the actively sustained humming sound. Enjoy the physical sensations that accompany the interplay of movement and vibration.

Step 4: Working with Pitch

Select a comfortable starting pitch in your middle voice. Allow a simple *huh* sound to fall from your body on your selected starting pitch each time you loop to the center. Lower the pitch a half step. Allow a simple *huh* sound to fall from your body each time you loop to the right. Lower the pitch a half step. Allow a simple *huh* sound to fall from you body each time you loop to the left (see Figure 11.5). Lower the pitch a half step. Allow a simple *huh* sound to fall from your body each

		1st Loop	2nd Loop	3rd Loop
3 LOOPS	Center	* HUH + MMMMMMMMMMMMMMMMMMMMMMMM		
3 LOOPS	Right	* HUH + MMMMMMMMMMMMMMMMMMMMMMMM		
3 LOOPS	Left	* HUH + MMMMMMMMMMMMMMMMMMMMMMMM		
3 LOOPS	Center	* HUH + MMMMMMMMMMMMMMMMMMMMMMMM		

* = receive a new breath

Figure 11.4 Carrying the Sound

		Descending/Ascending Pitches	Ascending/Descending Pitches
3 LOOPS	Center	Starting Pitch	Starting Pitch
3 LOOPS	Right	Lower Pitch ½ Step	Raise Pitch ½ Step
3 LOOPS	Left	Lower Pitch ½ Step	Raise Pitch ½ Step
3 LOOPS	Center	Lower Pitch ½ Step	Raise Pitch ½ Step
3 LOOPS	Right	Raise Pitch ½ Step	Lower Pitch ½ Step
3 LOOPS	Left	Raise Pitch ½ Step	Lower Pitch ½ Step
3 LOOPS	Center	Raise Pitch ½ Step (Starting Pitch)	Lower Pitch ½ Step (Starting Pitch)

* = receive a new breath

Figure 11.5 Working with Pitch

time you loop to the center. Repeat the looping sequence again, as-cending the musical scale until you return to your starting pitch. Rest. Repeat the entire sequence again, this time ascending and then de-scending the musical scale. Avoid pushing when ascending the scale or pressing when descending the scale.

Now explore the musical scale as explained above while carrying a simple humming sound as illustrated in Step 3.

Cross-legged Loop

See Figures 11.6, 11.7, and 11.8.

Step 1: Basic Exercise
This exercise uses the same basic looping action explored in the pre-vious exercise but in a cross-legged position. Your body's weight is distributed evenly over your pelvis. Your knees are bent and your ankles are crossed one on top of the other—right over left or left over

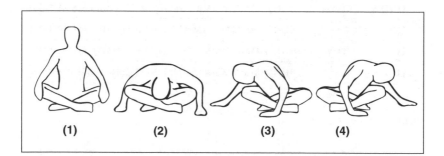

(1)   (2)   (3)   (4)

Figure 11.6 Basic Exercise: Cross-Legged Loop

		LOOP DOWN	LOOP UP	LOOP DOWN	LOOP UP	LOOP DOWN	LOOP UP
3 LOOPS	CENTER	*EE	*	EE	*	EE	*
3 LOOPS	RIGHT	AH	*	AH	*	AH	*
3 LOOPS	LEFT	OO	*	OO	*	OO	*
3 LOOPS	CENTER	EE	*	AH	*	OO	*

* = receive a new breath

Figure 11.7 Falling on EE AH OO

right. Your legs rest easily in the thigh socket. Your pelvis and spine are vertical and upright. Your rib cage and your head balance evenly and comfortably over your pelvis. Encourage the sensation of your whole torso lengthening and widening.

Step 2: Release—Sound Falls from the Body
Repeat the basic exercise. Allow a forward *ee* (as in *me*), an open *ah* (as in *ma*), and a full *oo* (as in *moo*) to fall from your body while looping, as illustrated in Figure 11.7.

Step 3: Charge—Body Carries the Sound
Repeat the basic exercise. Allow a forward *ee* (as in *me*), an open *ah* (as in *ma*), and a full *oo* (as in *moo*) to be carried by your body while looping, as illustrated in Figure 11.8. [The pitch selected for Steps 2 and 3 should be near the center of your vocal range—comfortably in your middle voice. (You should sense the possibility of notes above and below your starting pitch.) The sensation of your body carrying the sound should accompany the actively sustained vowel sounds. (When looping on the forward *ee*, enjoy a free play of vibration in your head and face. Allow the sound to fall directly into the front of your mouth onto your hard palate, teeth, and lips. When looping on the open *ah*, enjoy a sense of expanse in your mouth and throat. When looping on the full *oo*, enjoy the depth and weight of the sound vibrating in your chest.)]

Step 4: Working with Pitch
Steps 2 and 3 may now be explored on various pitches in your vocal range. The progression of the musical scale is the same as in the previous exercise.

		Loop Down	Loop Up	Loop Down	Loop Up	Loop Down	Loop Up
3 LOOPS	CENTER	*EEEEEEEEEEEEEEEEEEEEEEEEEEEEEEEEEEEEEEEEEEEE					
3 LOOPS	RIGHT	* AAAAAAAAAAAAAAAAAAAAHHHHHHHHHHHHHHHHH					
3 LOOPS	LEFT	* OOOOOOOOOOOOOOOOOOOOOOOOOO)OOOOOOO					
3 LOOPS	CENTER	* EEEEEEEEEE + AAAAAAHHHHH + OOOOOOOOOO					

* = receive a new breath

Figure 11.8 Carrying EE AH OO

Cross-legged Loop with Arms

See Figures 11.9, 11.10, and 11.11.

This is a variation of the previous exercises. Three looping actions with an undercurve toss of the arm are performed on the right side and then on the left side. (Sensing that the arm is being tossed by the looping action of the pelvis ensures its fluid integration with the pelvis, rib cage, and head.)

Step 1: Basic Exercise

1. Begin in the cross-legged sitting position. Rotate your pelvis, torso, and head to the right.

2. Crease your thigh socket, looping your pelvis, rib cage, and head downward over the right leg and foot. As your upper body loops downward, allow your left arm and hand to move in an undercurve scooping-like action along the floor on the right side of your body.

3. When the loop has completed its full outward trajectory, decrease your thigh socket so that your pelvis, rib cage, and head loop upward. As your upper body loops upright, your extended left arm is tossed upward toward the ceiling.

4. The loop is complete when your left arm falls in toward the center of your body.

Repeat three times. Rotate your pelvis to the left. Repeat three times.

Step 2: Release—Sound Falls from the Body

Repeat the exercise. Receive a new breath at the top of each phrase as your pelvis initiates the first looping action. Allow a forward *ee* to fall from your body on the first loop (see Figure 11.11), an open *ah* on the second loop, and a full *oo* on the third loop. (Receive a new breath each time your body loops upward. The sound falling from your body should be in the center of your vocal range—comfortably in your middle voice. You should sense the possibilities of notes above and below your starting pitch.) The sensation of your body yielding to gravity should accompany the passive release of your voice. Integration has been achieved when the release of the body, breath, and voice seem inseparable.

Figure 11.9 Looping with the Arm

		1ST Loop		2ND Loop		3RD Loop	
3 LOOPS	**RIGHT**	*	EE	*	AH	*	OO
3 LOOPS	**LEFT**	*	EE	*	AH	*	OO

* = receive a new breath

Figure 11.10 Falling EE AH OO

Step 3: Charge—Body Carries the Sound

Repeat the exercise. Allow your body to carry the forward *ee* into the open *ah* and finally into the full *oo* sound in uninterrupted and connected sequence while looping, as illustrated in Figure 11.11. The sensation of your body carrying the sound should accompany the actively sustained vowel sounds.

(When sequencing from *ee* to *ah* to *oo*, encourage the efficient and fluid movement of all the moveable parts of your mouth and throat. Ideally, all three vowels should have a forward, open, and full resonance. Focus on moving from vowel sound to vowel sound without any significant deterioration or abrupt shift in tonal quality or color.)

Step 4: Working with Pitch

You can now explore this exercise on various pitches in the vocal range. The progression of the musical scale is the same as in previous exercises.

		1st Loop	2nd Loop	3rd Loop
3 LOOPS	Right	* EEEEEEEEEE + AAAAAAHHHHHH + OOOOOOOOOOO		
3 LOOPS	Left	* EEEEEEEEEE + AAAAAAHHHHHH + OOOOOOOOOOO		

* = receive a new breath

Figure 11.11 Carrying EE AH OO

Looping with Vowels and Consonants

In celebrating the importance of vowel sounds, care must be taken not to neglect and shortchange consonant sounds. Clear and effective vowel and consonant sounds are equally essential to the expression of thought and feeling. It is often said that *feeling* is expressed through the open and expansive vowels and that *thought* is expressed through the dexterity and clarity provided by the consonants. Consonants reign in the boundless vowels, giving language shape and definition. When focusing on vowel sounds, freedom and fluidity are needed throughout the resonator. Consonants, on the other hand, require flexibility and dexterity. The physical and robust nature of consonants is often feared because it is thought they may somehow distort or interrupt the free and fluid resonance of the vowels, when in fact the proper shaping of the vowel space is improved by good consonants.

Using the same basic looping action as in the previous exercise, this exercise explores lip consonants, tip-of-the-tongue consonants, and palatal consonants.

Step 1: Basic Exercise

1. Lip consonants are made when the lips come in contact with each other. Repeat the basic looping exercise integrating the *ee*, *ah*, and *oo* sounds with the lip consonants *m*, *b*, *p*, and *w*, as illustrated in Figure 11.12.

2. Tip-of-the-tongue consonants are made when the tip of your tongue comes in contact with your gum ridge. Repeat the basic looping exercise, integrating the *ee*, *ah*, and *oo* sounds with the tip-of-the-tongue consonants *d*, *t*, *s*, and *z*, as illustrated Figure 11.12.

		1st Loop	2nd Loop	3rd Loop
Lip Consonants				
3 LOOPS	Right	* MEE	* MAH	* MOO
3 LOOPS	Left	* BEE	* BAH	* BOO
3 LOOPS	Right	* PEE	* PAH	* POO
3 LOOPS	Left	* WEE	* WAH	* WOO
Tongue-Tip Consonants				
3 LOOPS	Right	* DEE	DAH	DOO
3 LOOPS	Left	* TEE	TAH	TOO
3 LOOPS	Right	* SEE	SAH	SOO
3 LOOPS	Left	* ZEE	ZAH	ZOO
Palatal Consonants				
3 LOOPS	Right	* GEE	GAH	GOO
3 LOOPS	Left	* KEE	KAH	KOO
3 LOOPS	Right	* ngEE	ngAH	ngOO
3 LOOPS	Left	* JEE	JAH	JOO

* = receive a new breath

Figure 11.12 Consonants

3. Palatal consonants are made when the body of your tongue comes in contact with the roof of your mouth. Repeat the basic looping exercise integrating the *ee*, *ah*, and *oo* sounds with the palatal consonants *g*, *k*, *ng*, and *j*, as illustrated in Figure 11.12.

Step 2: Working with Pitch
Each of these consonant exercises can be explored on various pitches in the vocal range. The progression of the musical scale is the same as in previous exercises.

Step 3: Variations
Consonants may be explored after the vowel (*eem*, *ahm*, *oom*) or on both sides of the vowel (*meem*, *mahm*, *moom*).

Arched and Rounded Yawn/Sigh

See Figure 11.13.

Before beginning an advanced workout of your upper and lower voice, it is useful to stretch your vocal tract through a simple yawing/sighing action while arching and rounding the spine.

Step 1: Basic Exercise

1. Begin in the cross-legged sitting position. Tilt your pelvis backward and downward, allowing your whole spine to round.

2. Once in the rounded position, reverse the action; tilt your pelvis forward and upward, lengthening your spine and returning it to its upright and vertical position.

3. From this upright and vertical position, tilt your pelvis forward and downward, arching your spine.

Repeat this arching and rounding action three times. Rest.

During the arching and rounding actions, allow your jaw to swing freely from your head and spine. In the arched position, your lower jaw will drop down away from your upper jaw, creating a wide opening in your mouth and throat. In the rounded position, your lower jaw will swing upward near your upper jaw, creating a narrower opening in your mouth and throat.

Corresponding movement in your arms accompanies the arching and rounding action of your spine. As your spine rounds backward, your arms are naturally drawn in toward the center of your body. Your

Figure 11.13 Basic Exercise: Yawn/Sigh

arms bend slightly at the elbows and float upward in front of your body. The palms of your hands face inward toward your chest. As the spine arches, your arms extend outward and away from the sides of your body at approximately a 90-degree angle.

Step 2: Adding a Yawn/Sigh

Repeat the exercise. When your spine reaches its most arched position and your jaw falls into its most open position, allow your breath to release on a voiceless *hah* sound. Think of it as a *yawning/sighing action*. Yawning encourages expansiveness and openness in your mouth and throat. Sighing encourages the free and fluid release of your outgoing breath. Receive a new breath as your spine rounds. Repeat this arching and rounding action three times. Rest.

Side Loop with Arm Toss (Lower Voice) (Advanced)

See Figures 11.14, 11.15, and 11.16.

This exercise consists of three looping actions to the right and left sides, performed with an overcurve arm toss.

Step 1: Basic Exercise

1. Begin in the cross-legged sitting position. Allow your right arm to float upward above your head. Your elbow should be loose, not locked. Avoid lifting the shoulders. Your elevated arm should be placed slightly forward and in the front of your body.
2. In a sideways looping action, allow your pelvis to toss your rib cage, head, and arm over to the left.
3. After looping a comfortable distance over to the left, allow your pelvis to toss your rib cage, head, and arm back to their initial upright and vertical position.

Repeat three times on the left side. Repeat three times on the right side. Rest. The weight of your upper body should not collapse or drop when lowered to the side. Encourage a sense of expansiveness and openness in your rib cage. Your pelvis remains anchored to the floor to provide a stable base of support.

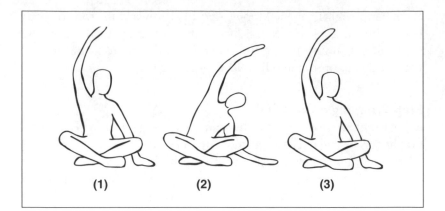

Figure 11.14 Basic Exercise: Side Loop

Step 2: Release—Sound Falls from the Body
Repeat the exercise. Select a comfortable starting pitch in your lower voice. (The specific pitch doesn't matter as long as it does not produce strain.) Allow an *oh, oo,* and *ah* sound (as in m*ow*, m*oo*, and m*a*) to fall from your body each time you loop to the side, as illustrated in Figure 11.15. The sensation of your body yielding to gravity should accompany the passive release of the vowel sounds.

Step 3: Charge—Body Carries the Sound
Once again, select a comfortable starting pitch in your lower voice. Repeat the exercise, allowing your body to carry the *oh, oo,* and *ah* sounds in uninterrupted and connected sequence, as illustrated in Figure 11.16. Focus on moving from vowel sound to vowel sound without any significant deterioration or abrupt shift in tonal quality or color. The sensation of your body carrying the sound should accompany the actively sustained vowel sounds.

Step 4: Working with Pitch
Beginning on a comfortable pitch in your lower voice, move down the musical scale in half steps each time you repeat the *oh, oo,* and *ah* vowel sequence. When you explore the pitches of your lower voice, the sound may either fall from your body or be carried by your body. It is possible to extend your lower voice to an almost inaudible, rumbling sound without damage or strain. Only go as low as you can without

		1st Loop	2nd Loop	3rd Loop
3 LOOPS	Right	* OH	* OO	* AH
3 LOOPS	Left	* OH	* OO	* AH

* = receive a new breath

Figure 11.15 Falling into the Lower Voice

		1st Loop	2nd Loop	3rd Loop
3 LOOPS	Right	* OOOOHHHH + OOOOOOOOOOO + AAAAAAHHHHHH		
3 LOOPS	Left	* OOOOHHHH + OOOOOOOOOOO + AAAAAAHHHHHH		

* = receive a new breath

Figure 11.16 Carrying the Lower Voice

pushing or pressing. Legitimate increases in range are always a by-product of economy and ease. In time and with repetition, your lower voice will be freed and strengthened.

As the pitch moves lower:

- Encourage a sense of expansion in your mouth and throat.
- Encourage a sense of release in the energy of your body.
- Allow your body to move more slowly. Thought and feeling are typically revealed at a slower pace in your lower voice than they are in your upper voice.
- Sense the weight of your body becoming heavier to encourage greater solidity and depth in tonal quality and color.

Forward Loop with Arm Toss (Upper Voice) (Advanced)

See Figures 11.17, 11.18, and 11.19.

This exercise consists of three forward looping actions performed with an overcurve arm toss.

Step 1: Basic Exercise
1. Begin in a seated position with your pelvis tilted downward and backward. Allow your whole spine to round. Bend your arms at your elbows and let them float upward in front of your body. The

palms of your hands face your chest. Your knees are bent slightly, and the soles of your feet rest comfortably on the floor.

2. Crease your thigh sockets, looping your pelvis, rib cage, head, and arms forward, up and over your legs and feet.

3. When the loop has completed its full forward trajectory, de-crease your thigh sockets so that your pelvis, rib cage, head, and arms loop upward.

Repeat this looping action three times.

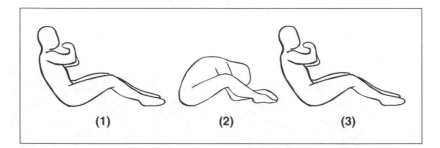

Figure 11.17 Basic Exercise: Forward Loop

		1st Loop	2nd Loop	3rd Loop
3 LOOPS	FORWARD	* MEE	* MAY	* MY
3 LOOPS	FORWARD	* MEE	* MAY	* MY
3 LOOPS	FORWARD	* MEE	* MAY	* MY

* = receive a new breath

Figure 11.18 Falling into the Upper Voice

		1st Loop	2nd Loop	3rd Loop
3 LOOPS	FORWARD	* MMMMEEEE + MMMMAAAAYYYY + MMMMMYYYYY		
3 LOOPS	FORWARD	* MMMMEEEE + MMMMAAAAYYYY + MMMMMYYYYY		
3 LOOPS	FORWARD	* MMMMEEEE + MMMMAAAAYYYY + MMMMMYYYYY		

* = receive a new breath

Figure 11.19 Carrying the Upper Voice

Step 2: Release—Sound Falls from the Body

Select a comfortable starting pitch in your upper voice. The specific pitch doesn't matter as long as it doesn't produce strain. Repeat the exercise. Close your lips and hum the selected note up into your head. Allow the *me, may,* and *my* sounds to fall from your body each time you loop forward, as illustrated in Figure 11.18. Rest. The sensation of your body yielding to gravity should accompany the passive release of the vowel sounds.

Step 3: Charge—Body Carries the Sound

Once again, select a comfortable starting pitch in your upper voice. Repeat the exercise. Carry the *me, may,* and *my* sounds in an uninterrupted and connected sequence, as illustrated in Figure 11.19. Focus on moving from vowel sound to vowel sound without any significant deterioration or abrupt shift in tonal quality or color. The sensation of your body carrying the sound should accompany the actively sustained vowel sounds.

Step 4: Working with Pitch

Beginning on a comfortable pitch in the upper voice, move up the musical scale in half steps, raising the pitch each time the *me, may,* and *my* vowel sequence is repeated. When you explore the pitches of your upper voice, the sound may either fall from your body or be carried by your body. Allow the momentum created by the looping action in your body to help you access your upper voice. Don't reach or strain for the higher notes. At the first sign of tightening or constricting in the throat, return to a more comfortable pitch and start again.

As the pitch moves higher:

- Encourage a sense of expansion in your mouth and throat.
- Encourage a sense of charge in the energy of your body.
- Allow your body to move more quickly. Thought and emotion are typically revealed at a faster pace in your upper voice than they are in your lower voice.
- Sense the weight of your body becoming lighter to encourage greater brilliance and radiance in tonal quality and color.

Loop-Sit Loop (Horizontal Vocal Freedom) (Advanced)

See Figures 11.20 and 11.21.

This exercise consists of five forward looping actions performed with an undercurve arm toss. It develops your ability to move from vowel sound to vowel sound on any single note in your vocal range without any significant changes in tonal quality and color.

Step 1: Basic Exercise

1. Sit on the floor with your body's weight equally distributed over your pelvis. Allow your legs to rest comfortably on the floor. Your knees are straight but not locked and face the ceiling. Your pelvis, rib cage, and head are vertical and upright. Your rib cage and head balance evenly and comfortably over your pelvis. Encourage the sensation of your whole torso lengthening and widening.

2. Crease your thigh sockets, looping your pelvis, rib cage, and head downward over your legs and feet. As your upper body loops forward and downward, allow your arms and hands to slide out across the floor along the outside of each leg.

3. When the loop has completed its full forward trajectory, de-crease your thigh sockets so that your pelvis, rib cage, and head loop upward and your extended arms are tossed up toward the ceiling.

4. Complete the loop by rounding your spine and letting your arms fall in toward the center of your body.

Repeat five times.

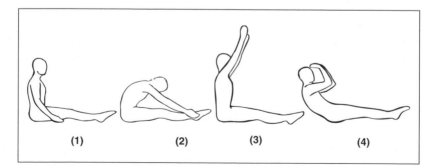

Figure 11.20 Basic Exercise: Looping in Long-Sit

Step 2: Working with Pitch

Repeat the exercise. During the first loop, beginning on a comfortable starting pitch in your middle voice, allow your body to carry your voice on an *ee* sound (as in *me*) changing to an *ay* sound (as in *may*) changing to an *ah* sound (as in *ma*) changing to an *oh* sound (as in *mow*) changing to an *oo* sound (as in *moo*) in an uninterrupted and connected sequence as illustrated in Figure 11.21. Lower the pitch one half step and repeat the process. Continue down the scale into your lower voice as far as is comfortable. Rest. Reverse the process and work back up the scale to your starting pitch. Rest. Repeat the entire five-vowel sequence again, raising the pitch in half steps as far as is comfortable. Reverse the process and move back down the scale to your starting pitch. Focus on moving from vowel sound to vowel sound without any significant deterioration or abrupt shift in tonal quality or color. The sensation of your body carrying the sound should accompany the actively sustained vowel sounds.

Loops with Undercurve and Overcurve Arm Tosses (Vertical Vocal Freedom) (Advanced)

See Figures 11.22–11.25.

This exercise consists of two forward looping actions, the first loop performed with an undercurve arm toss, the second with an overcurve arm toss. It develops your ability to move through a series of connected notes in your vocal range on a single vowel sound without any significant or abrupt changes in tonal quality or color.

Step 1: Basic Exercise

1. Sit on the floor with your body's weight equally distributed over your pelvis. Allow your legs to rest comfortably on the floor. Your knees are straight but not locked and face the ceiling. Your pelvis,

Undercurve Loop	* EEEE + AAAYYY + AAAHHH + OOOHHH + OOOO	Pitch Change
Undercurve Loop	* EEEE + AAAYYY + AAAHHH + OOOHHH + OOOO	Pitch Change

* = receive a new breath

Figure 11.21 Horizontal Vowel Freedom

rib cage, and head are vertical and upright. Your rib cage and head balance evenly and comfortably over your pelvis. Encourage the sensation of your whole torso lengthening and widening.

2. Crease your thigh sockets, looping your pelvis, rib cage, and head downward over your legs and feet. As your upper body loops forward, allow your arms and hands to slide out across the floor along the outside of each leg.

3. When the loop has completed its full forward trajectory, de-crease your thigh sockets, looping your pelvis, rib cage, and head upward. As your upper body loops upright, your extended arms are tossed upward toward the ceiling.

4. Complete the loop by rounding your spine and letting your arms fall in toward the center of your body.

5. Begin the overcurve arm toss where the undercurve arm toss ended.

6. Crease your thigh sockets, looping your pelvis, rib cage, head, and arms upward. As your upper body loops upward, your extended arms are tossed upward toward the ceiling.

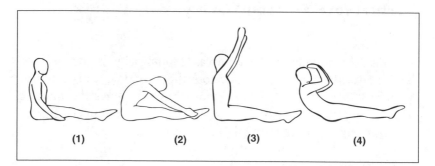

Figure 11.22 Basic Exercise: Undercurve Loop with Arm

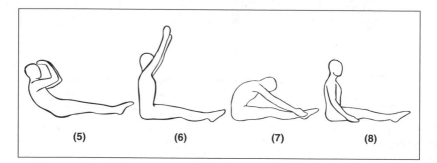

Figure 11.23 Basic Exercise: Overcurve Loop with Arm

7. As your upper body continues to loop up and over your extended legs and feet, allow your arms to fall forward along the outside of each leg near the floor.

8. When the loop has completed its full forward trajectory, decrease your thigh sockets, returning your pelvis, rib cage, and head to their initial starting position.

Repeat the entire double looping sequence five times.

Step 2: Working with Pitch (Arpeggio)

Repeat the exercise using an arpeggio scale (see Figure 11.24). Begin on a comfortable pitch in your middle voice. Allow your body to carry an *ee* sound (as in *me*) on an arpeggio scale during the first under- and overcurve loops. Lower the pitch one half step. Repeat on *ay, ah, oh,* and *oo* sounds (as in *may, ma, mow, moo*), lowering the pitch one half step each time the vowel sound is changed (as illustrated in Figure 11.25). Reverse the sequence by returning up the scale in half steps to your starting pitch. Rest. Repeat, moving up the scale into your

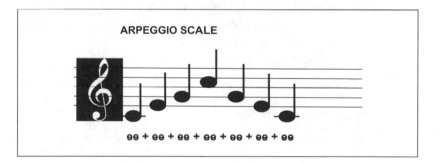

Figure 11.24 Arpeggio

1st Loop	* EEEEEEEEEEEEEEEEEEEEEEEEEEEEEEEEEEEEE	1st Arpeggio
2nd Loop	* AAAAAAAAAAAAAAAAYYYYYYYYYYYYYYYYYY	2nd Arpeggio
3rd Loop	* AAAAAAAAAAAAAAAAHHHHHHHHHHHHH	3rd Arpeggio
4th Loop	* OOOOOOOOOOOOOOHHHHHHHHHHHHH	4th Arpeggio
5th Loop	* OOOOOOOOOOOOOOOOOOOOOOOOOOOOO	5th Arpeggio
	Undercurve Toss of the Arm	Overcurve Toss of the Arm	

* = receive a new breath

Figure 11.25 Arpeggio

upper voice and back down the scale to your starting pitch. Focus on moving up and down the musical scale on each vowel sound without any significant deterioration or abrupt shift in tonal quality or color. The sensation of your body carrying the sound should accompany the actively sustained vowel sounds.

Stride-Sitting Loop (Five-Note Scale) (Advanced)

See Figures 11.26–11.29.

This exercise consists of three looping actions, the first two performed with an undercurve arm toss, the third with an overcurve arm toss.

Step 1: Basic Exercise

1. Sit on the floor with the weight of your body equally distributed over your pelvis. Your legs and feet lengthen comfortably in the front of your body in a V. Your knees are straight but not locked and face the ceiling. Your pelvis, rib cage, and head are vertical and rotated to the side. Your rib cage and head balance evenly and comfortably over your pelvis. Encourage the sensation of your whole torso lengthening and widening.

2. Crease your thigh sockets, looping your pelvis, rib cage, and head over your right leg and foot. As your upper body loops forward, allow your left arm and hand to slide out across the floor along the inside of your right leg.

3. When the loop has completed its full outward trajectory, de-crease your thigh sockets so that your pelvis, rib cage, and head loop upward. As your upper body loops upright, your extended right arm is tossed toward the ceiling.

4. Complete the loop by rounding your spine and letting your right arm fall in toward the center of your body.

5. Repeat. Then begin the overcurve-arm-toss loop where the undercurve-arm-toss loop ended.

6. Crease your thigh sockets, looping your pelvis, rib cage, head, and arm upward.

7. As your upper body continues to loop up and over your right leg and foot, allow your arm to fall forward along the inside of your right leg near the floor.

Figure 11.26 Basic Exercise: Loop in Stride 1

Figure 11.27 Basic Exercise: Loop in Stride 2

8. When the loop has completed its full forward trajectory, de-crease your thigh sockets, returning your pelvis, rib cage, and head to their initial starting position.

Repeat the entire sequence on the left side. Rest.

Step 2: Working with Pitch

Now explore the exercise using a five-note scale (see Figure 11.29). Begin on a comfortable pitch in your middle voice. As your voice progresses through the five-note scale, allow your body to carry the *ee, ay,* and *ah* vowel sounds (as in *me, may,* and *ma*) on the first undercurve loop, the *oh, oo,* and *oh* vowel sounds (as in *mow, moo,* and *mow*) on the second loop, and the *ah, ay,* and *ee* vowel sounds (as in *ma, may,* and *me*) on the third loop as illustrated in Figure 11.29. When the five-note scale is completed, lower the pitch one half step and repeat the looping action on the left side. Repeat several times, moving into your lower voice as far as is comfortable. Then return up the scale to your starting pitch. Rest. Repeat, this time exploring your upper voice. Focus on moving from vowel sound to vowel sound and

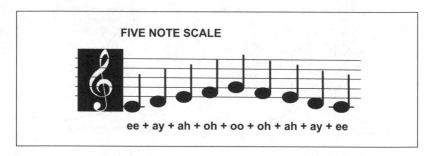

FIVE NOTE SCALE

ee + ay + ah + oh + oo + oh + ah + ay + ee

Figure 11.28 Five-Note Scale

*EE	AY	AH	OH	OO	OH	AH	AY	EE
1st Undercurve Loop			2nd Undercurve Loop			3rd Undercurve Loop		
Five half-steps up the scale					Four half-steps down the scale			

* = receive a new breath

Figure 11.29 Loop in Stride (table)

note to note without any significant deterioration or abrupt shift in tonal quality or color. The sensation of your body carrying the sound should accompany the actively sustained vowel sounds.

Step 3: Five-Note Scale with Vowels and Consonants

Explore the stride-sitting loop exercise using various consonant sounds before, after, and on both sides of the vowel sounds.

12 Standing Exercises

In an hourlong workout, approximately fifteen or twenty minutes should be devoted to standing exercises, which are of two types: *stationary* and *locomotive*. The stationary exercises explore upright movement while standing more or less in one spot. The locomotive exercises involve traveling across the floor. In a traditional technique class, the lying and breathing and sitting and sounding exercises remain relatively consistent. The standing exercises, however, are always different and constantly evolving.

There are two reasons for this. First, your voice and body fail to get a complete workout if too much time is spent learning new exercises. New exercises are not necessarily better exercises. A great deal can be learned by repeating the same well-developed sequence of exercises again and again. Second, it is important to have some variety. Learning to pick up new combinations of movement, different sequences of vowel and consonant sounds on a variety of pitches in your vocal range, is liberating and keeps your voice and body supple and attentive. With time and experience, the standing exercises can become quite complex and full of adventure.

Unfortunately, most standing exercises are too complex to describe fully in writing. Instead, I will outline a series of guidelines to help you create your own. Many of the previous lying and breathing and sitting and sounding exercises can easily be modified into standing exercises. Anyone with an imagination and an intuitive sense of the physical can create a flexible and challenging set of standing exercises.

Students with a background in dance have a clear advantage here. Those with little dance experience are without question charting new and unfamiliar territory. However, these on-your-feet explorations are not about dance but about the integrated use of your voice and body in preparation for human expression. Many times students with little or no dance experience create the most inventive and useful standing exercises. Though many combinations of movement may mirror those in a dance class, others may look nothing like traditional dance movement.

Standing exercises are usually created in several steps:

1. *The physical phrase.* Begin by creating a repeatable phrase of movement. Ideally, all standing exercises should explore energy (charge/release), size (expand/contract), progression (center/periphery), orientation (contact/withdraw), and free flow. Your legs and feet may be arranged in a variety of configurations: first position, second position, fourth position, parallel, in rotation. Explore a full range of motion in all the various joints of your body—bending, rotating, swinging, lifting, extending, rounding, spiraling, tossing, pointing, flexing, and so forth. Explore walking, running, sliding, lunging, jumping, leaping, hopping, skipping, galloping, turning, spinning—any type of advancing or retreating movement that propels your body forward or backward in space.

2. *The breath and the body.* Repeat the physical phrase several times. Where in the phrase can the breath fall from your body? Where in the phrase do you want to receive a new breath? Can your body carry your breath over the entire phrase? Repeat the phrase alternating between allowing the breath to fall from your body and be carried by your body.

3. *Sound and movement.* Repeat the physical phrase several times. Where in the phrase can the sound fall from your body? Can your body carry the sound over the entire phrase? Repeat the phrase alternating between allowing the sound to fall from your body and be carried by your body.

4. *Vowels and consonants.* Select a vowel or a series of vowels to explore. If you like, add any consonant or consonant combinations before or after any or all of the vowel sounds. Explore language:

"Mary Had a Little Lamb," Shakespeare, Mamet, any memorized or improvised piece of text.

5. *Range.* Select a pitch or series of pitches to explore. You may want to limit your exploration to your middle, lower, or upper voice. Explore a simple musical scale: triad, five-note, arpeggio, anything you like. Explore a phrase from a song ("Twinkle, Twinkle, Little Star," "Michael, Row Your Boat Ashore") or a series of randomly selected improvisatory pitches.

These directives are by no means definitive but rather a jumping-off point. Moving while making sound is an exhilarating physical experience. Freedom, spontaneity, and creativity facilitate a liberating and pleasurable exploration and extension of your voice and body.

First-Function
Improvisation

These improvisational studies seek to help you integrate and organize a wide variety of emotional, mental, and physical sensations into meaningful expressive action. They are designed to cultivate a healthy respect for impulse, spontaneity, and creativity while simultaneously expanding and broadening the actor's imagination and increasing expressive power. The improvisational studies foster an intuitive and nonintellectual approach to skill building. The studies begin with the repetition of a physical action and progress sequentially adding breath, then sound, and finally words and phrases. The outcome is the organized, sensuous, and integrated expression of the body's most powerful thoughts and feelings. The improvisational studies have proved to be an essential link in bridging the wide gap that so often separates traditional methods of voice, movement, and acting training. Through the improvisations, the actor learns new forms of expression never thought possible and many of which he or she has never experienced in his or her own life. In an advanced study, specific improvisational studies can be structured to address individual deficiencies and limitations. The goal is to develop an instrument that is flexible and dynamic and in direct contact with pure sensation. In Chapter 2, we discovered that there are two ways to know something—a *thinking way* and a *sensing way*. Consequently, there are two ways to approach improvisation. You can begin by *thinking*—exploring an expressive action in its second function; or you can begin by *sensing*—exploring an expressive action in its first function. Consider these examples:

1. Suppose you are given the following set of circumstances:

   > You have overslept. You are late for work for the third time this week. You cannot find your car keys. Go.

   If, after thinking for a moment, you begin to search frantically for the car keys, you are taking the second functional approach, exploring expressive action through an intellectual analysis of the relevant circumstances. The mind prompts or motivates your body to integrated expressive action.

2. Alternately, suppose you are asked to move in an empty space in the following manner:

   Energy: Charged

   Direction: Indirect

   Focus: Sharp

   If, without thinking, you begin to move frantically around the room in a manner similar to someone "searching" for their car keys, you are taking a first-functional approach. The body, not the mind, prompts or motivates you to integrate expressive action. Later someone asks, "What are you doing?" and you respond, "I'm searching for my car keys."

These two distinct starting points, physical and intellectual, illustrate the fundamental differences between improvisation in its first and second function. Regardless of the starting point—physical or mental—an improvisation is successful when your body and mind unite to play a meaningful expressive action.

The improvisational studies presented here explore, in one form or another, an *expressive action in its first function*. Typically, when improvising in the first function, you will be asked to explore, develop, and repeat a single expressive action. You will not be asked to group a series of expressive actions into a larger context or story.

Additionally, you will not be asked to answer such questions as, "Who am I? Where am I? what do I want?" or to explore other intellectual aspects of the action: "My character is adopted, my character is afraid, my character is a habitual liar." Rather you will be encouraged to explore the action physically without analysis, interpretation, or justification. By momentarily putting your intellect on hold, you will be encouraged to focus on the physical life of the expressive action: Does my body feel *heavy* or *light*? Am I moving *fast* or *slow*? Does my body *expand* or *contract*? Am I *charging* or *releasing*? Free of character scenario, situation, and circumstance, the process of expression is explored *in and of itself and for its own sake*. Emphasis is placed on spontaneity, exploration, emotion, structure, form, technique, and execution. The goal is to develop a specific set of physical resources that lead, prompt, and motivate expressive action. With repetition and practice, you will begin to view your body as a rich physical and psychological playground. Many times your body will prompt you to undertake new and unfamiliar expressive actions that were previously unthinkable.

Improvising in this manner is like *falling in love in the abstract*. The gentleman who falls in love in the abstract loves the sound of the young woman's voice, the color of her hair, the twinkle in her eye— all her physical attributes—without any intellectual knowledge of who she is or where she came from. Similarly, when improvising in the first function, the actor falls in love with the expressive action in the abstract—its *weight, direction, flow, energy, orientation,* and *size*—all the physical properties that give it its unique form and character.

When improvising in this abstract manner, you are not exploring a specific expressive action linked to a specific character, time, or place but a universal expressive action that transcends character, time, and place. It's as if you are playing the expressive action in every context, in every time, in every place, in every situation, as every character. What emerges is an archetypical understanding of an expressive action in its purest form.

Typically, if you can play an expressive action in the first function, you'll have little problem translating, adjusting, or modifying the expressive action to meet the needs of a specific character in a play. The adjustments needed to play the same expressive action in Shaw, Shakespeare, Ibsen, Pinter, Miller, or Mamet are relatively easy to make. Furthermore, because all expressive actions have a universal structure (they all *charge* and *release, contact* and *withdraw, expand* and *contract,* and so on) when you learn to play one expressive action, your body and voice are simultaneously programmed to play all expressive actions.

When you are improvising in the first function, your body, not your mind, leads and directs the exploration. Mental activity is not encouraged or emphasized. When you direct your attention to your physical experience, however, you cannot simply turn off your brain and make it quit thinking. As soon as you begin to explore the expressive action physically, your mind will begin thinking, rationalizing, and organizing the expressive action into some type of logical and meaningful human experience. Context, motivation, and justification emerge spontaneously because of the expressive action itself, not from any predetermined deliberation or analysis on your part. Sometimes the physical sensations created will remind you of past events. Other times, the intellect suggests possible scenarios that transcend personal experience.

Inherent within all of us is a built-in type of physical and emotional memory that is more powerful, clear, and profound than we may have previously thought. An expressive action has a mystical and transformative narrative power. When an expressive action is played *in and of itself and for its own sake,* meaning and context emerge naturally and effortlessly.

Language

When improvising in the first function, you will most often begin with a physical and vocal exploration of an expressive action without using language. When the expressive action is fully realized, you will be asked to find a piece of text to explore while playing it. This process is the reverse of what typically goes on in acting classes and in rehearsals. Most often the actor begins with the language provided by the playwright and looks for an expressive action appropriate for the text. However, a great deal can be learned about both expressive action and language by occasionally working the other way around.

Once an actor realizes the expressive action in the body, I often ask her or him to compose a spontaneous piece of text that seems appropriate. Sometimes I ask other students in the class to improvise a piece of text for the student exploring the expressive action. Additionally, the expressive action might be played while speaking a nursery rhyme or while reciting the words to the song "Happy Birthday" or while counting from 132,256 to 132,262. In other instances, I take lines from actual scripts. It is important to include a great variety of playwrights and writing styles—the more the better. I often ask improvising students if they can remember a line or two from a play they know that is particularly suited to the expressive action they are playing. Sometimes other students in class provide lines from scripts. Most important, exploring one expressive action using several pieces of text of various lengths keeps the actor from falling into an arbitrary line reading that is disconnected from the physical sensations experienced in the body. The intellectual power of words must not be allowed to stifle the sensations created in the voice and body by the expressive action.

Basic Exercise

Improvising in the first function is traditionally broken down into five separate steps, which are explored sequentially:

> Step 1: Prompt.
>
> Step 2: Phrasing.
>
> Step 3: Action.
>
> Step 4: Breath and body.
>
> Step 5: Sound and movement.

Exploring an expressive action step by step like this is a type of research in which the physical properties of an expressive action are investigated in your body, breath, and voice. The goal is to arrive at a rich, full-bodied expressive action that is deeply rooted in sensation.

Initially, you are encouraged to progress through each of the steps sequentially, moving to the next step only when an experiential understanding of the current step is fully realized. When it feels right, it usually is right. Intuition, sensation, and experience are the best guides for when to move forward. Repeat each of the steps numerous times as needed. Repetition is essential to learning. Each time the expressive action is repeated, its physical and emotional life is clarified in your body, breath, and voice. An experienced actor can move through each of the steps quite quickly. In advanced study, steps may even be skipped or their order changed. However, when difficulty arises, a more structured and systematic exploration may be required.

The explanations below incorporate fictitious stories about how I might work with a student. While these stories may seem contrived and pedantic, they paint a clear picture of how the improvisational studies are structured.

Step 1: Prompt

An improvisation begins with a specific prompt to spark the imagination and serve as a physical point of departure. Sometimes the actor is asked to play an expressive action that is *indirect, charged,* or *diffused*. Commonly, prompts are stated in the form of a verb: *to slash, to tease, to demean,* or *to reject*. (An exhaustive verb list is provided in the appendix.) A great variety of other types of prompts may be used, including idiomatic expressions: *to give someone the evil eye, to cry bloody murder,* or *to keep a stiff upper lip*. Any point of departure is acceptable, so long as it suggests a clear physical activity that prompts an integrated expression of thought and feeling.

Let's look at an example. I give Steve the prompt *to bang*. He accepts the prompt, stands, and wanders around the room for a few moments looking perplexed, clearly trying to think of something to do. I ask, "Does the prompt motivate you to any type of physical action?" Steve looks more confused and thinks for a while longer. Then he turns around quickly, looks at the door, and asks, "Who's there?" I have Steve repeat this activity several times and then ask, "What just happened?" He replies, "Someone banged on the door, and I was just checking to see if anyone was there." I respond, "You have just played the expressive action *to check,* not *to bang*. You were checking, not banging. The door was banging. Can you bang?"

I tell Steve he is thinking too much. He has intellectually scripted a door-banging scenario but hasn't explored the prompt physically. Steve looks perplexed: "So what *do* I do?" I respond, "Why don't you begin to move around the room, and when you're ready allow the banging action to happen in your body and go from there. The banging you are looking for is a physical action that contains and reveals thought and feeling." Steve seems encouraged. He begins to walk around the room. Eventually, with a fair amount of force, Steve runs into the wall. I smile and tell him to continue but not to hurt himself. Steve runs into the wall several more times. Now the movement does appear to contain and reveal thought and feeling. Steve is frustrated and distraught each time he bangs into the wall. This is an important first step in the exploration. Steve is well on his way to finding a playable expressive action.

"What are you doing?" I ask. Steve responds defiantly, "I'm banging into a wall." "Yes," I say, "you are literally banging into a wall. Can you think of the wall as a metaphor for a type of human behavior?" He responds, "Yes, it's like I'm beating my head against the wall." "Very good, but you don't need a wall to do that do you?" I ask. He says no and begins to walk around the room. Eventually, he stops, lifts up both hands near his face, and calls out, "I can't take this anymore." I ask him to repeat the action several times. He does. I tell Steve he has successfully played an expressive action. He smiles and asks, "But did I play the expressive action *to bang*?"

I'm somewhat confused: "Didn't you?" He responds, "Well, I said I was beating my head against the wall, not banging." "Does it matter?" I ask. He says, "I guess not." I explain that as long as we arrive at a physical action that contains and reveals thought and feeling, the improvisation has been successful.

Steve has successfully taken the journey from prompt to expressive action. In time and with experience, this process will become quick and less labored. Steve is just beginning to learn the ins and outs of improvising in the first function. It is important to remember that the prompt is not the expressive action but rather a starting point that *leads to* expressive action. It stimulates the actor to expressive action; it doesn't dictate or prescribe a specific result.

Different actors respond differently to different prompts. Oftentimes, two actors can take the same prompt and arrive at two completely different expressive actions. Sometimes the prompts are successful; sometimes they are less successful. What stimulates the imagination of one actor often does not stimulate the imagination of another. What is important is that the prompt motivate the actor to some type of physical action. In time and with consistent practice, most actors can take almost any prompt and allow it to lead and direct them to a playable expressive action.

Step 2: Phrasing

Once the prompt has motivated the actor to a playable expressive action, that action needs to be phrased. This is very similar to the verbal phrasing of a sentence. A well-phrased sentence progresses naturally and fluidly—word by word—toward the verbal expression of a complete thought and feeling. Similarly, an expressive action progresses naturally and fluidly—weight shift by weight shift—toward the physical expression of a complete thought and feeling.

Work on phrasing is largely work on *rhythm*: the progressive orderly flow with which an expressive action begins, develops, and subsides. When an expressive action is well phrased, it has a rich rhythmical life. Phrasing is essentially organizing a weight shift or a series of weight shifts into a single phrase that has a clearly defined beginning, middle, and end. We are very aware of how a sentence begins and ends on the page but less aware of how a thought and a feeling begins and ends in the body. When and where does the movement begin? How does it develop and mature? When and how does it resolve, end, or fade away? These are the essential physical questions to be explored in the body when working on phrasing.

Ultimately, successful phrasing occurs when a series of expressive actions are strung together one right after the other in a seamless, fluid, and uninterrupted manner. Ideally, each expressive action should flow naturally and rhythmically into the next like a series of consecutive waves of the ocean. Scientists describe the two essential points on a wave as the *crest* (the high point) and the *trough* (the low point) (see Figure 13.1). Learning to sequence one expressive action after another is largely learning to ride the crest and rest in the trough, to balance the seamless sequence of activity and passivity, doing and nondoing, motion and rest—the natural ebb and flow of life. Like the waves of the ocean, expressive actions do not always come in regular intervals. Some days the tides are choppy and quick, other times the swells are long and slow with much time in between one wave and the next.

Again, let's look at phrasing in action. Sonya has received a prompt and has organized it into playable expressive actions. I ask her to repeat her expressive actions several times. She does. She is clearly having trouble with phrasing. She starts and stops in an arbitrary way that looks more like an exercise than natural human behavior. I say, "Your rhythm seems very choppy. Can you structure each expressive action in your body so that it has a clearly organized beginning, middle, and end?"

Sonya responds, "I know what the expressive action is. I sense it and feel it. I just have difficulty organizing it."

I say, "Each expressive action has its own rhythmical life, but finding this life will require some exploration in your own body. The rhythm of an expressive action is similar to the rhythm of your breath. There is a need for breath. The breath comes. The breath goes. There is a rest. And the whole cycle repeats. The expressive action should come and go in the same way." She plays her expressive action several more times. I suggest she is rushing.

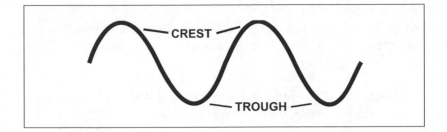

Figure 13.1 Wave

Sonya says, "It is like I just get nervous and I end the expressive action before it has completely resolved and then I feel like I should be doing something and I start again before I am ready."

"Give the expressive action all the time that it needs," I reply. "Direct your attention to how each expressive action begins and ends. Often when an expressive action begins and ends naturally, everything else seems to fall into place."

Sonya asks, "How does an expressive action begin and end?"

I suggest this is a difficult question to answer, but I provide the following suggestions to help her. "With respect to initiating the action, does the impulse for expressive action spring from something that is going on inside you—*withdraw*—or is it motivated by something going on outside of you—*contact*?" Sonya says the motivation for her expressive action is prompted by a series of internal sensations. I suggest that she attend to these sensations before initiating the expressive action. "You seem to start the expressive action arbitrarily and mechanically. Can you wait for an impulse to begin?"

"Yes, but how long can I wait?" she asks.

"Until the impulse for a new action comes."

"How do I know it will come?"

"New impulses always come. Just like your next breath always comes. Your job is simple. Wait and direct your attention toward your internal sensations until you feel the desire to express yourself. Now, with respect to ending the action, does it turn off rather quickly like flipping off a light switch, or does it fade away more slowly like turning down a dimmer switch on a chandelier?" Sonya states it turns off quickly. "Great, so when you're finished, you're finished. Do not linger or second-guess the end of your action. When you are finished, let it go. Then rest and repeat the expressive action again." She plays her expressive action sequence several more times. The rhythm and the phrasing are much improved.

Step 3: Action

Having found a playable and repeatable well-phrased expressive action, the actor is encouraged to investigate the physical properties that define its essential structure:

- *Energy*: Where do I feel a charge in my body? Where do I feel release?
- *Orientation*: When do I contact the outside world? When do I withdraw?
- *Size*: When does my body expand? When does my body contract?
- *Progression*: How does the action move from the center of my body to the periphery?
- *Flow*: Is the action free or bound? Am I holding myself back or letting myself go?

The manner in which the minor properties of an expressive action—direction, speed, weight, control, and focus—affect the quality and character of the expressive action may also be explored.

Let's say Jan is playing the expressive action *to snap*. She has received the prompt, organized it into a well-phrased expressive action, and scripted an appropriate piece of text. The expressive action looks something like this: she gets a disgusted grimace on her face and quickly turns her head and snaps, "Damn, Janet! Enough already!"

Progression: Center/Periphery

I ask Jan to play her action several times. She does. I observe that the lower half of her body is stationary and disconnected. Jan simply turns her head and snaps. Everything from the head down is immobile. I ask, "Where in your body do you feel the action is centered?"

Jan pauses and responds, "In my pelvis."

I suspect she thinks that is what I want to hear, that like a good and conscientious student she wants to please. "Are you sure?" I ask. I tell her to repeat the expressive action several times. She does and then says: "The action is centered in my head."

This is an important discovery. "Yes," I say, "is it possible that your whole body could snap and not just your head?" She says yes and repeats the expressive action. This time the movement begins in her pelvis and her whole body seems to snap. The expressive action is full-bodied, more committed, and the size of the thought and feeling being expressed is more powerful. Jan repeats this centered action several times. She asks, "Which is right?"

I respond, "They are both right. The body organizes thought and feeling in many ways. In general, important, committed, and spontaneous expression engages the whole body and moves outward from the pelvis to the head, arms, hands, legs, and feet." I ask her to play the expressive action several more times, alternating between centering the action in the pelvis and centering the action in her head. She does. I ask her what she has discovered.

"They're both real. The centered one is just more intense and powerful."

Flow: Free/Bound

I respond, "Is there any difference in the flow of these expressive actions? Is one more *free* or *bound* than the other?"

Jan knows the answer to this question immediately. "When the expressive action is centered in my head, I tend to hold of the rest of my body back. I feel tenser. It's like I don't want my whole body to do anything, because yelling and moving at the same time seems so rude. When I move from my center, my whole body follows and plays the expressive action. I really snap and it's intense. Which is right?"

I tell her, "Just be yourself. It is only pretend. We can be rude when improvising and not worry about the consequences. Both options have a unique place in the larger context of human expression. If it is important to you not to be rude, I suspect the expressive action centered in your head is best. However, if you really want to make your point and communicate the depth and richness of your thoughts and feelings, the expressive action centered in your pelvis is probably your best bet."

Size: Expand/Contract

Jan repeats the expressive action again, alternating between centering it in her pelvis and centering it in her head. I now direct her attention to the relative degree of expansion and contraction in her body. "What did you discover?"

"My body expands as I express myself and contracts when I am finished. When I expand, my left arm reaches out like I am trying to push someone away."

"Is there a difference when the action is centered in your pelvis and when it's centered in your head?"

"Yes. When the expressive action is centered in my head, tension keeps my body from expanding like it does when the expressive action begins in my center."

Energy: Charge/Release

"Is any of this related to the manner in which the energy charges and releases in your body?" I ask.

"Yes, it seems all connected. When I expand, the energy in my body charges, and when I contract, the energy in my body releases, but when my body is tense and I am holding back, I do not feel I release as much. It seems like I kinda hold the feeling when I hold my muscles, and I feel kinda frustrated."

"So freely expressing the feeling is more pleasurable?"

Jan giggles. "Yes, but it is such a negative feeling, I would not have thought so."

"I think we always feel better—at least on some level—when we express our thoughts and feelings, regardless of whether we perceive them as positive or negative."

Orientation: Contact/Withdraw

"Talk to me about contact and withdraw," I say.

"That is very simple. I contact when I express myself and withdraw when I'm finished."

"Very good," I say, "I think it's just that simple. The expressive action *to snap* has very strong contact. However, other expressive actions like *to shy away, to cower,* or *to retreat* might be organized very differently. Sometimes we express ourselves when we make contact, and other times we express ourselves when we withdraw."

Jan sits down.

"Tell me more about your expressive action."

"It's like Janet is just getting on my nerves so I just snap." [Remember, her text was: "Damn, Janet! Enough already!"]

"Do you know Janet?" I ask.

"No," she says, "the only thing I can think of is that my brother used to tell a joke whose punch line was 'Damn, Janet.'"

"Do you know anything else about why you snapped at Janet?" I ask.

"It wasn't just one thing. When I was repeating the expressive action, all kinds of things came to my mind. Like she was bugging me to loan her money or wanted to know if I liked a boy—crazy stuff—some of my thoughts made sense, some of them didn't. Sometimes I was just so focused on how I was snapping that I didn't have time to think about why I was snapping."

"So you simply played the expressive action in and of itself and for its own sake?"

"Yes, and whatever came up, came up. Sometimes I was furious and other times really vulnerable and hurt. It was often very different. It kept shifting and changing."

"We have been focusing on the expressive action in its first function; consequently, clear intellectual answers about why we are playing the expressive action are secondary and less important than discovering things about the physical life of the expressive action in the body," I say. "Can you tell me something about the action in the first function?"

"Yes. It is very charged, short, direct, and stable, but mostly has really strong contact . . . and I would not say it's heavy, but it certainly is not light."

Step 4: Breath and Body

Now the actor is ready to explore how the breath and body integrate in expressive action. Remember, breath is the framework and foundation for sound. When the action of the breath is fully integrated with the action of the body, the foundation is laid for the successful transition into integrated vocal action. The goal is to allow the outgoing breath to respond and intermingle with the movement of the body.

Release—Breath Falls from the Body

Matt has taken a prompt, organized it into a playable expressive action, and scripted a preliminary piece of text. The expressive action looks something like this: Matt, in a full-bodied physical gesture, lifts up both arms and hands. As the arms and hands release downward Matt states, "I'm sorry . . . really . . . really . . . sorry." Matt plays his expressive action several times.

I ask, "Are you expressing yourself on the *charge* or the *release*? Do you feel that your thoughts and feelings fall *from your body*, or are they *being carried by your body*?"

He says, "They fall." Indeed, the words just cascade out of his mouth.

We begin to work with the breath. I ask him to put the text away for a while and just explore the physical phrase. He repeats the expressive action without the text. "Where does your body release?" I ask.

"When I take a step forward and lower my arms."

"Very good. Now when your body releases, can you explore allowing the breath to fall from your body as well?"

As the energy in his body releases, his breath releases on a simple sigh, a voiceless *huh* sound. The release of the breath and the release of the body are seemingly inseparable. He repeats this several times. He begins to settle more fully into the sensation. I ask him to alternate between releasing the breath and speaking the text. He does this several times. The expressive action becomes deeper and more committed. "What is different?" I ask.

"I feel like when I release my breath I get more in touch with my feelings, so when I switch and speak the text, it is more vulnerable and committed."

"Yes, but every expressive action organizes the breath energy differently. Sometimes the organization of the breath energy in the body makes us feel more aggressive, introspective, or energized. It is always very different. The wonderful thing about the breath is that it often puts us directly in touch with our feelings."

Charge—Body Carries the Breath

Julie has received a prompt and organized it into a playable expressive action that looks something like this: she lifts both arms out in front of her body and takes several steps backward. Her action is methodical and measured. Her eyes are intense and beaming. She is clearly expressing a thought and feeling. She has not yet composed a piece of text for this action. I ask, "What are you doing?"

Julie responds, "I'm not sure."

"What does it feel like?"

"I just move backwards in a slow, stable way with sharp focus. Like I'm backing down . . . sorta . . . no, it's more like I am washing my hands of all this mess." She repeats the action several more times.

"Do you feel that the expressive action *falls from your body* or is being *carried by your body*?" I ask.

"It is carried. My body is charged the whole time that I step backward."

"Very good. Now as your body charges, can you explore allowing the body to carry the breath on a simple hiss—a voiceless *sss* sound?" Julie carries a simple *sss* sound over the entire physical phrase. The physical sensations in her body mix and mingle and ride on the outgoing breath. You can hear the slow, stable, sharp quality in the action of her breath. I ask her to repeat the expressive action several times. She does.

When she finishes, Julie says: "Each time I repeated the expressive action, I took a different number of steps backward. I just took however many steps I felt were right for the expressive action, and each time my body seemed to know how much breath I needed. I always had enough breath, and I never had to think about it."

"This is exactly the kind of integration of moving and breathing that we are looking for," I say.

Step 5: Sound and Movement

When a healthy integration of the breath and body has been achieved, the final step is to explore sound. When working with sound and movement, expressive actions are played on any vowel sound or any combination of vowel and consonant sounds, but using words is strictly prohibited. When introduced inappropriately, the intellectual nature of language can render an expressive action lifeless and dull. Oftentimes, the sensual and physical life of the voice and body is stymied or lost in a torrent of thoughts and words. Sounding and moving without using language returns the actor to a primal and reflexive method of communication that is visceral and full-bodied and linked directly to impulse.

Language began with primitive sound and movement explorations. When a sound kept its meaning beyond its initial instinctive utterance, language was born. Exploring the voice in this "prespeech" way gives us a greater appreciation of how physical sensations in the body influence and affect the sound of the voice. When we are moving and sounding in an integrated manner, even the most subtle and nuanced shifts in the body manifest themselves in the sound of the voice. The goal is to allow the expressive action to place the voice in the body. When this occurs, we *hear* the voice through the body. The feelings in the body are imprinted on the voice and travel outward on resonant sound waves to reveal the emotional state of the speaker. The voice is best viewed as the oral extension of the body—it is through the voice that the body speaks.

Release—Sound Falls from the Body / Charge—Body Carries the Sound

Jon has taken the prompt *to plod* and arrived at a repeatable and playable expressive action: he plods around the room in a released, slow, and heavy manner. In the course of the exploration, he has composed a piece of text: "So why is everybody always picking on me." This vocal expression is playful, endearing, and lighthearted, yet Jon is plodding. I have him play the expressive action several times. There seems to be a disconnect between his body and his voice. The text seems divorced and isolated from the physical action. The body seems alive and expressive, but the text is arbitrary and contrived. Each time Jon repeats the action, he mechanically emphasizes different words. "*Why* is everybody always picking on *me*?" "Why is *everybody* always picking on me?" "Why *is* everybody always picking on me?" The result is pedantic and stilted.

"The expressive action seems to be fully expressed in your body," I suggest, "but I'm having trouble with the language. Could you try to settle more fully into the sensation? How does this slow, released, heavy 'plodding action' affect your voice?"

He repeats the expressive action several times. I suggest that he put the text away for a while and just work with sound and movement. We select an *oo* vowel. With the language out of the way, the sound begins to integrate with the plodding action of his body. Each time there is a weight shift in his body, there is a corresponding shift in the sound of his voice. "Does the sound fall from your body or is the sound carried by your body?" I ask.

"I'm not exactly sure. I feel like the sound falls from my body each time I take a step, but I also feel like my body carries the sound over the entire plodding action."

"I think you're right," I say. "While some expressive actions clearly *fall from the body* and others are clearly *carried by the body*, with others it can be difficult to tell. What we have here is a very complex organization of energy. First explore the expressive action by allowing an *oo* sound to fall from your body, then carry the *oo* sound and see what you discover." Jon does so. Both appear to be working equally well, and it is difficult to distinguish between the two. I ask, "Do you have any idea whether your expressive action is more *charged* or more *released*?"

"Yes," said Jon. "It's difficult to tell, but I think it's more released."

I ask Jon to alternate between playing the action on the *oo* sound and playing it while speaking the text, encouraging him to speak the text with the same sound qualities that his body experienced when working with the *oo* sound. He achieves a fine level of integration. "Why is everybody always picking on me?" seems to plod along as he moves around the room. I ask what he discovered.

"I was thinking about the words so much that all the extra mental effort was disconnecting me from my body. When it was really working, I felt like the text and sound were coming out of my whole body and not just my brain."

A Dozen Suggestions

The following suggestions, though not absolute rules, have proved useful when improvising in the first function:

1. Work in an empty space without props, furniture, or costumes. The body should be the sole means and method of expression.

2. Remember that there is a fundamental difference between *repeating a movement* and *playing an expressive action*. Each time an expressive action is repeated, although the quality of the movement should be somewhat similar, the expressive action itself is always varied and flexible. Just as no two moments in life are the same, no two expressive actions are the same.

3. Avoid playing physical states, such as *tired, drunk, dizzy,* or *stoned.* These involuntary physical conditions impede the expression of thought and feeling rather than help it.

4. Avoid playing emotional states, such as *sadness, joy,* or *anger.* Feeling must always be the indirect *result* of the expressive action.

5. Avoid miming absent objects. Car doors, apples, toothpicks, and playing cards are not an essential component of any expressive action and are unnecessary in improvisation.

6. Avoid actions that require a partner, such as handshakes, punching, caressing, or tickling. While these actions certainly contain and reveal thought and feeling, they can only be practiced effectively with a partner. (However, it is useful to direct your expressive action toward an imaginary *listener*, in much the same way you would when auditioning or performing a monologue.)

7. Do only what is essential—avoid any unnecessary movement or gestures. Streamline the expressive action. You only need the activity that is *essential* for the expression of thought and feeling. Extraneous movement or vocal activity only creates interference and muddies the character of the expression action.

8. Finish your business—play your expressive action completely. Continue to play the expressive action until the thought and feeling has been fully expressed. For example, if you are *pleading,* continue *to plead* until your message has been heard. If you are

warning, continue *to warn* until the warning has been heeded. This helps ensure that your actions have a clearly defined beginning, middle, and end.

9. Complete all weight shifts—don't become entangled in incomplete or muddied physical action. When the movement of the body is clarified, thought and feeling are also clarified.

10. Use universal expressive actions. Look for universal expressive actions that have been played in all times by all people in all places.

11. Move first, think second. It is not necessary to have any preconceived mental notions about how to play any given expressive action. Simply explore the expressive action in your body. This type of nonintellectual exploration is similar to a musician playing with musical notes to create a melody or a dancer playing with movement to create a piece of choreography. The process is intuitive and experiential.

12. Have fun. Playfulness is key. A spirit of play sets up a creative, impulsive, nonjudgmental environment for improvisation.

The improvisational studies presented in the subsequent chapters are by no means exhaustive. Improvisation by nature is flexible and adaptable. The possibilities are virtually limitless. There are so many vast and varied expressive actions and different ways of exploring them that it would be impossible to exhaust all possibilities here. My suggestions are a point of departure. Once the basic structure is understood, new and different improvisational studies may be created and existing ones may be easily modified or adapted.

14 Foundational Exercises

Swarming

Before beginning to improvise in the first function, it's a good idea to explore the physical properties of an expressive action in this simple exercise. (Its name is taken from the way in which bees swarm around their hive.)

Step 1

Move from the middle of the room outward to any point along any one of the four sides of the room. After arriving at this outermost point, change direction and return to the center of the room. Once back at the center, repeat this swarming action to and from other outermost points for a minute or so.

Step 2

Explore each of the physical properties of an expressive action (listed below) one at a time as you swarm around the room. For example, swarm in a very *charged* manner for several moments, then in a very *released* manner, and so on, until each property has been explored. It is not necessary at this point to develop your exploration into a playable expressive action. Focus instead on the contrasting physical sensations created in your body.

- *energy*: charge/release
- *orientation*: contact/withdraw
- *size*: expand/contract
- *progression*: center/periphery
- *flow*: free/bound
- *direction*: direct/indirect
- *speed*: fast/slow
- *weight*: light/heavy
- *control*: stable/unstable
- *focus*: sharp/diffused

Exploring Physical Phrasing

A well-structured physical phrase is essential to successful improvisation; it is the foundation for the expression of thought and feeling. Physical phrasing is essentially organizing a weight shift or a series of weight shifts that make up an expressive action into a single phrase that has a clearly defined beginning, middle, and end. Phrasing an expressive action is similar to phrasing any physical activity. Examining a series of simple physical actions will give you a clearer understanding of how expressive action is organized into physical phrases.

Select one of the following physical activities:

- Pour a drink of water.
- Scratch your head.
- Turn a page of a newspaper.
- Cross and uncross your legs.
- Fold a letter.
- Button a sweater.

Repeat the activity several times, taking a short rest or pause between each repetition. Allow the activity to become fluid and seamless, structuring it so that it has a very clearly defined beginning, middle, and end. Where does the action begin in your body? How does the activity escalate and develop? When does it diminish and dissolve? Repeat using the other physical activities listed above or any physical activities you choose.

Exploring Idiomatic Expressions

Each of the idiomatic expressions listed below describes an emotional state in terms of various parts of the body as well as certain bodily functions. Working with idiomatic expressions solidifies the important role your body plays in the expression of feeling and is a useful starting point when learning to improvise in the first function.

Step 1: Prompt

Select one of the idiomatic expressions listed below. Allow the physical exploration of the idiomatic expression to develop into a playable expressive action. Repeat this expressive action several times.

lose your head

save face

face up to

grit your teeth

give your eyeteeth

be a pain in the neck

shoulder a burden

twist someone's arm

get your nose out of joint

be nosey

can't stomach something

be a tight ass

get out of hand

turn the other cheek

be starry-eyed

have an ace up your sleeve

slap someone down

lower your sights

be a sight for sore eyes

have no balls

get pissed off

get choked up

shrug it off

be itching to do something

be able to breathe again

have your heart set

be full of hot air

have your nose in the air

roll in the aisles

run around in circles

have your tongue a-wagging

be empty-handed

get back on your feet

have your back to the wall

turn your back

bad-mouth

have a bad taste in your mouth

beat your brains out

bend over backward

be on bended knee

put your best foot forward

be too big for your britches

swallow a bitter pill

draw a blank

bleep something out

turn a blind eye

cry bloody murder

blow off steam

blow your cork

get the blues

talk a blue streak

feel it in your bones

dig in your heels

be bored stiff

beat your brains out

rack your brain

put on a brave face

hold your breath

bite the bullet

burst at the seams

bust a gut

button your lip

raise your eyebrows

get something off your chest

chew out

keep your chin up

have a chip on your shoulder

lick your chops

keep a civil tongue

have your head in the clouds

get cold feet

be hot under the collar

cool your heels

crack a smile

get the creeps

cross your heart

cross your fingers

get your dander up

be dead on your feet

turn a deaf ear

be tickled to death

throw your hands up

be driven up the wall

drop in your tracks

give someone the evil eye

prick up your ears

eat your heart out

have stars in your eyes

eye someone

keep a straight face

find it in your heart

be full of hot air

give a tongue-lashing

tear your hair out

sit on your hands

wash your hands of someone

bite someone's head off

stick your head in the sand

hold your head up

hold your tongue

jump out of your skin

keep a stiff upper lip

kick up your heels

laugh something off

lie through your teeth

look down your nose

feel your blood run cold

feel your mouth water

don't believe your eyes

stay on your toes

let your heart go out to
someone

quake in your boots

shoot your mouth off

Step 2: Phrasing

Continue to explore the physical life of the expressive action by allowing it to develop into a well-structured physical phrase that has a clearly defined beginning, middle, and end.

Step 3: Action

Repeat the expressive action several times and become aware of its physical life in your body. How would you describe your expressive action in its first function? Can you identify three or more physical properties (such as charged, stable, and direct) that seem most pronounced in your expressive action?

Step 4: Breath and Body

Explore one of the following while playing your action:

- Release: breath falls from the body on a simple sigh—a voiceless *huh* sound.
- Charge: the body carries the breath on a simple hiss—a voiceless *sss* sound.

Repeat until the movement of your body and the movement of your breath seem inseparable.

Step 5: Sound and Movement

Explore one of the following while playing your actions:

- Release: sound falls from the body on any selected vowel sound.
- Charge: the body carries the sound on any selected vowel sound.

Repeat until the movement of your body, breath, and your voice seem inseparable.

Step 6: Language
Improvise your expressive action using various pieces of text.

Step 7: Repetition
Repeat with as many idiomatic expressions listed above as spark your imagination.

Exploring Physical Properties

Explore a single physical property of an expressive action.

Step 1: Prompt
Select a physical property of an expressive action to explore. Allow the physical property to develop into a playable expressive action. For example: *indirect* might develop into the expressive action *to wander*; *heavy, to plod*; or *fast, to zip*.

Steps 2–6 (as listed on pages 155–156)

Step 7: Repetition
Repeat with the remainder of the physical properties.

Stacking

Explore working with several physical properties of an expressive action simultaneously.

Step 1: Prompt
Select three physical properties of an expressive action (*free, stable,* and *light,* for example). Begin moving around the room in a *free* manner. When you are ready, add (or *stack*) *stable* and begin moving in a *free* and *stable* manner. When you are ready, add (or *stack*) *light* and begin moving in a *free, stable,* and *light* manner. Develop this *free, stable* and *light* movement into a playable expressive action. Repeat this action several times.

Steps 2–6 (as listed on pages 155–156)

Step 7: Repetition

Repeat the stacking exercise several more times exploring different physical properties.

Exploring Verbs

Step 1: Prompt

Select a verb from the list in the appendix, and allow the prompt to develop into a playable expressive action.

Steps 2–6 (as listed on pages 155–156)

Step 7: Repetition

Repeat many times exploring other verbs on the list in the appendix.

Switching

Switch or rotate physical properties while playing a single expressive action.

Step 1: Prompt

Select a verb from the list in the appendix, and allow the prompt to develop into a playable expressive action.

Steps 2–6 (as listed on pages 155–156)

Step 7: Switching

Now play the expressive action in a very *charged* manner. Allow the quality and character of the expressive action to change or modify as necessary. Switch to *released*. Again, allow the expressive action to change or modify as necessary. Now switch to *contact*. Switch to *withdraw*. Switch to *expand*. Switch to *contract*. Switch to *center, periphery; free, bound; direct, indirect; fast, slow; heavy, light; stable, unstable; sharp, diffused*.

Step 8: Repetition

Repeat several more times exploring other verbs selected from the list in the appendix.

Sequencing

A *sequence* is a series of expressive actions played one right after another with a brief rest or pause between each action. Begin by moving from one end of the rehearsal studio to the other in a relatively straight line, subdividing this across-the-floor movement into a series of segments or phrases. For example, take five steps forward. Rest. Now take three steps forward. Rest. Now take eight steps forward. Rest.

Step 1: Prompt
Travel across the floor again in the 5-3-8 step pattern above, remembering to rest in between each of the three phrases. Select a different physical property of an expressive action to explore during each of the three phrases. For example, on the *first five-step phrase,* explore *slow.* On the *second three-step phrase,* explore *indirect.* On the *third eight-step* phrase, explore *heavy.* Repeat several times. Allow the movement in each of the three phrases to develop into a playable expressive action.

SLOW	INDIRECT	HEAVY
5 STEPS (REST)	3 STEPS (REST)	8 STEPS (REST)

Steps 2–6 (as listed on pages 155–156)
Repeat each step while traveling across the floor in the 5-3-8 step pattern. The phrase need not have any logical order that tells a story or makes intellectual sense.

Step 7: Repetition
Select a new group of physical properties to explore, varying the number of steps in each of the phrases.

Segueing

Segue is a musical term meaning to continue without interruption or pause (pronounced: seg-way). Play a series of expressive actions one right after another *without* resting or pausing between them but rather connecting them to form a single phrase containing multiple actions that have a clearly defined beginning, middle, and end.

Step 1: Prompt

Select five verbs from the list in the appendix (*to oppose, to thrust, to haggle, to babble,* and *to pounce,* for example). Allow the physical exploration of these five verbs selected to develop into five playable expressive actions.

Steps 2–6 (as listed on pages 155–156)

Repeat each step for each of the five actions you selected.

Step 7: Segue

Now segue from one action to the next without pausing in between, creating one unified longer phrase that has a clearly defined beginning, middle, and end:

1ST ACTION	2ND ACTION	3RD ACTION	4TH ACTION	5TH ACTION
TO OPPOSE +	TO THRUST +	TO HAGGLE +	TO BABBLE +	TO POUNCE

This phrase need not have a logical order that tells a story or makes intellectual sense.

Step 8: Repetition

Repeat with other groups of verbs selected from the list in the appendix.

Dynamic (Delicate Through Strong)

The *dynamic* is the degree of intensity with which an expressive action is played. Certain expressive actions have a high dynamic—*to explode* or *to scream bloody murder.* Other expressive actions have a low dynamic—*to tiptoe* or *to whisper.* Expressive actions with a high dynamic are referred to as *strong.* Expressive actions with a low dynamic are referred to as *delicate.* Many expressive actions (*to plead, to warn,* or *to beg,* for example) can be played with many dynamic variations. Therefore, it is useful to place *strong* and *delicate* on a scale from one to ten, one being the most delicate dynamic and ten being the strongest.

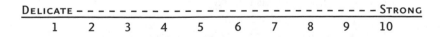

DELICATE – STRONG
1   2   3   4   5   6   7   8   9   10

Step 1: Prompt

Select a verb from the list in the appendix that can be played with a number of dynamic variations. Allow the verb to develop into a playable expressive action.

Steps 2–6 (as listed on pages 155–156)

Step 7: Dynamic Variation

Repeat the action five times, varying the dynamic each time. For example, the first time play the expressive action at a dynamic of nine, the second time at a dynamic of four, the third time at a dynamic of one, the fourth time at a dynamic of six, the fifth time at a dynamic of seven.

Step 8: Repetition

Repeat with other verbs selected from the list in the appendix.

Classifying Actions

Classifying expressive actions by category leads to a deeper understanding of the diverse and rich language used to describe the manner in which thoughts and feelings are expressed through physical action. It also helps you develop a useful vocabulary of verbs with which to label the physical life of a thought and feeling in the body.

Step 1: Prompt

For each of the following categories, select five verbs from the list in the appendix:

- *Emotional actions*: verbs referring to an emotional state or condition (*to lament, to despair, to delight, to brood, to bristle*).
- *Physical actions*: verbs referring to a physical action or movement (*to claw, to hobble, to knock, to dab, to slither*).
- *Intellectual actions*: verbs referring to a mental activity or state (*to criticize, to debate, to hypothesize, to discriminate, to rationalize*).
- *Intentional actions*: verbs referring to a desire, want, goal, or need (*to avoid, to debate, to wish, to halt, to quiz*).

- *Nonintentional actions*: verbs referring to passive, involuntary, or vegetative conditions (*to digress, to gawk, to sink, to tremble, to stagger*).
- *Manipulative actions*: verbs referring to deceptive or devious ways of controlling others (*to intimidate, to fib, to brainwash, to coerce, to mystify*).
- *Repressive actions*: verbs referring to the controlling or restricting of thought and feeling (*to cap, to hold in, to cower, to bite your tongue, to bind*).
- *Explosive actions*: verbs referring to violent or uncontrollable expression (*to explode, to vent, to boil, to lose it, to hit the ceiling*).
- *Exaggerated actions*: verbs referring to the disingenuous overplaying or embellishing of a real or pretended thought and feeling (*to lie, to embellish, to brag, to flatter, to patronize*).

Select one group of classified actions to explore, allowing them to develop into playable expressive actions.

Steps 2–6 (as listed on pages 155–156)
Repeat each step for each of the five actions you selected.

Step 7: Segue or Sequence
Segue the five expressive actions into one longer and continuous phrase, or sequence them as five shorter phrases with a pause in between each, or combine the two (for example, sequence the first three actions, then segue the last two actions).

Step 7: Repetition
Repeat with the remaining groups of classified actions.

Barre Exercises

A *ballet barre* is a handrail fixed to the wall in a dance studio at which the ballet dancer practices and repeats a series of steps that are committed to memory and practiced without the assistance of other dancers. Similarly, the expressive actor's barre is a series of expressive actions committed to memory and practiced in an empty studio without the assistance of other actors. The focus is on developing and maintaining a flexible and supple expressive instrument. Like the ballet barre, the actor's barre is designed to become a part of the actor's daily workout.

Classic Barre

This is a series of twenty expressive actions committed to memory and played one right after the other in a single exercise. Each of the twenty selected expressive actions explores one of the physical properties of an expressive action.

Step 1: Prompt
Pair a verb from the list located in the appendix with each of the physical properties of an expressive action. For example:

- *Energy*: charge: *to bark* / release: *to fumble.*
- *Orientation:* contact: *to meddle* / withdraw: *to cower.*
- *Size*: expand: *to surrender* / contract: *to sag.*
- *Progression:* center: *to wallow* / periphery: *to pester.*
- *Flow:* free: *to cruise* / bound: *to gnash.*
- *Direction:* direct: *to drill* / indirect: *to amble.*
- *Speed:* fast: *to lash* / slow: *to linger.*
- *Weight:* heavy: *to ram* / light: *to flitter.*
- *Control:* stable: *to thrust* / unstable: *to fumble.*
- *Focus:* sharp: *to glare* / diffused: *to zone out.*

Step 2
Develop each verb selected into a playable expressive action.

Step 3
Assemble the twenty expressive actions into the repeatable barre. You may structure the actions in any order you like. It is not necessary to structure the expressive actions in any logical order that makes intellectual sense or tells a story. The phrasing of the actions is also flexible and open to experimentation. For example, you can *sequence* through the expressive actions, resting between each one. However, you can also *segue* several actions together into a single phrase without resting in between (see pp. 155–156). The possibilities of phrasing are quite flexible and are virtually limitless.

Step 4: Repetition
- Repeat daily as a method of practice and preparation.
- Limit your practice to an exploration of your breath. As you play your barre, allow your breath to fall from your body or to be carried by your body.
- Limit your practice to an exploration of your voice. As you play your barre, allow your voice to fall from your body or to be carried by your body.

In time, it may be necessary to change several expressive actions or the way they are sequenced or segued to provide variety. When the possibilities for learning and development have run their logical course, construct a new barre and begin again.

Dynamic Barre

Explore each of the twenty expressive actions in your classic barre with dynamic variations. Play them all at a very low dynamic. Play them all at a very high dynamic. Play them all at a medium dynamic. Give each one a different dynamic. You may find it helpful to assign each expressive action a number one through ten, one being the most delicate dynamic and ten being the strongest dynamic (see pp. 159–160).

Extended Barre

This exercise can be performed successfully only when the classic barre is fully memorized and can be repeated without interruption or prompting. Select one physical property for extended exploration while you play your classic barre. (Certain expressive actions will change significantly and in many ways express new and different thoughts and feelings.)

Step 1: Prompt

Let's say you select *unstable* for extended exploration. Every action in your classic barre must now be played in an *unstable* manner. Your first expressive action must now be both *unstable* and *charged*, your second expressive action *unstable* and *released*, your third expressive action *unstable* and *expansive*, your fourth *unstable* and *contracted*, and so on. (With respect to control, a *stable* expressive action is already *stable* and can't be played as unstable, so it is omitted.) Here's a detailed breakdown:

- *Energy:* charge + unstable/release + unstable.
- *Orientation:* contact + unstable/withdraw + unstable.
- *Size:* expand + unstable/contract + unstable.
- *Progression:* center + unstable/periphery + unstable.
- *Flow:* free + unstable/bound + unstable.
- *Direction:* direct + unstable/indirect + unstable.
- *Speed:* fast + unstable/slow + unstable.
- *Weight:* heavy + unstable/light + unstable.
- *Focus:* sharp + unstable/diffused + unstable.

Step 2

Sequence or segue through each of the expressive actions in the classic barre in an unstable manner.

Step 3: Repetition
Repeat, substituting other first-functional properties as extensions.

Habitual/Nonhabitual Barre

At this point, you will have developed some experience and may perhaps have discovered that there are certain types of expressive actions you can play rather easily and other types you struggle with or avoid. With this information, you can now begin to focus more specifically on developing and stretching your expressive potential.

Step 1: Prompt
Select three physical properties that you are very comfortable organizing into playable expressive actions—habitual actions. Select three physical properties that you are uncomfortable organizing into playable expressive actions—nonhabitual actions. Pair each selected physical property with five verbs from the list in the appendix. For example:

Habitual properties:

> Fast: *to slash, to scramble, to nail, to shirk, to hustle*
>
> Light: *to prance, to josh, to admire, to skip, to flirt*
>
> Direct: *to challenge, to pester, to scold, to blast, to concentrate*

Nonhabitual properties:

> Slow: *to ponder, to creep, to hover, to haunt, to coax*
>
> Heavy: *to block, to pound, to demolish, to agonize, to sink*
>
> Indirect: *to wander, to stagger, to dodge, to frolic, to quibble*

Step 2
Sequence or segue through each of the expressive actions in the barre.

Step 3: Repetition
When the possibilities for learning and development have run their logical course, construct a new habitual/nonhabitual barre by selecting different comfortable and uncomfortable expressive actions for focused exploration.

Language and Character

A detailed study of language and character could easily fill up two separate books. This short chapter provides introductory remarks and offers preliminary exercises that shed light on how an expressive action influences language and character.

Expressive Action and Language

There is an old theatre joke in which two actors argue over how a character is to say a line. One insists it is "*Hark*, I hear the *cannons* roar"; the other insists it is "Hark, *I* hear the cannons *roar*." Neither line reading leads to satisfactory results and both actors are equally the butt of the joke (Hornby 1992).

Unfortunately, sitting down with a script and a pencil and making intellectual decisions about which words are important and should be given special vocal emphasis can lead to stilted and mechanical line readings. I call this misguided process *playing the text*. The problem is, this how-will-I-say-this-line approach can lead to an exploration of the intellectual power of the word at the expense of the experiential, sensorial, and emotional power of the body. The result is often all head and little heart. The actor's job is not merely to get the meaning of the language into the head but, equally important, to get the feeling of the language into the body.

When an actor merely *plays the text,* the line delivery is often pedantic, shallow, declamatory, and devoid of genuine feeling. The results are less than satisfying. "I *need* a vacation." "*I* hate *her.*" "Is *today* Wednesday?" The actor states, tells, emphasizes, stresses, and underscores the literal meaning of the text but expresses little else. Everything is rattled off as an intense statement of fact. A possible subtext for mechanical line deliveries like these could be *"I really mean it"* or *"Listen to what I'm saying."*

Without question, the intellectual meaning of the text can be understood by analyzing the structure of language. For example, it might be very helpful to recognize that the words *winter* and *summer* and *discontent* and *glorious* are used in opposition to create meaning in the opening soliloquy in *Richard III*:

Now is the <u>winter</u> of our <u>discontent</u>

Made <u>glorious</u> <u>summer</u> by this sun of York;

However, understanding the rhetorical structure of the text does not always ensure that the actor is expressing a feeling. It is fitting that we call the actor an *actor* and not an *orator* or a *reciter.* The job of the actor is not to set down clever and predetermined ways of turning a phrase but rather to find a series of expressive actions that indirectly play the words—as Hamlet's eloquent advice to the player suggests, "suit the action to the word and the word to the action. . . ."

Invariably the appropriate expressive action always emphasizes the appropriate words. Words and actions meet differently in every context. Almost any part of speech can be stressed: verbs, nouns, even pronouns, prepositions, and articles. The complexity of emphasis is linked directly to the expressive action and cannot be solely determined mechanically or intellectually. The subtleties and nuances of complex stress sometimes confound the intellect, transcend the literal, and run contrary to common sense.

Ultimately, the actor must explore the language of the play physically as well as mentally. This physical exploration of the text is rooted in sensation and expressive action. The actor relying on the vast power of the intuition develops a *sense*—a feeling—of how the words live in the body. When language is explored through the body, it evokes specific physical properties. Language can actually charge and release, contact and withdraw, expand and contract. It can be centered or peripheral, free or bound, direct or indirect, fast or slow, heavy or light, stable or unstable, sharp or diffused. Some thoughts race, soar, and expand; others slip away, dwindle, and subside; still others plod along in fits and starts—the possibilities are endless. In a good play, the skillfully structured language suggests specific physical sensations that lead and direct the actor toward the appropriate expressive action. This subtle and indirect, understated and undercelebrated communication between talented playwright and gifted actor is one of the most magical and mysterious aspects of theatrical collaboration.

Swarming Using Vowel Sounds

Before beginning your work with language, explore the physical properties of an expressive action on a series of vowel sounds.

Step 1: Swarming

Move from the middle of the room outward to any point along any one of the four sides of the room. After arriving at that outermost point, change direction and return to the center of the room. Once back at the center, repeat this swarming action to and from other outermost points for a minute or so.

Step 2: Moving and Sounding

As you swarm around the room, explore each of the physical properties of an expressive action (see below) with each of the following vowel sounds: *ee* (as in m*e*), *ay* (as in m*ay*), *ah* (as in m*a*), *oh* (as in m*ow*), *oo* (as in m*oo*). Allow the physical sensations in your body to shape and influence the quality and color of each of the vowel sounds.

- *Energy:* charge/release.
- *Orientation:* contact/withdraw.
- *Size:* expand/contract.
- *Progression:* center/periphery.
- *Flow:* free/bound.
- *Direction:* direct/indirect.
- *Speed:* fast/slow.
- *Weight:* heavy/light.
- *Stability:* stable/unstable.
- *Focus:* sharp/diffused.

It is not necessary at this point to develop your exploration into a playable expressive action.

Stacking

Explore several physical properties of an expressive action simultaneously.

Step 1: Stacking
Select three physical properties of an expressive action: *free*, *stable*, and
light, for example. Begin moving around the room in a *free* manner.
When you are ready, add (or *stack*) *stable*. Move in a *free* and *stable*
manner. When you are ready, add (or *stack*) *light*. Move in a *free*, *stable*,
and *light* manner.

Step 2: Moving and Sounding
As you move around the room in free, stable, and light manner, explore each of the following vowel sounds: *ee* (as in m*e*), *ay* (as in m*ay*),
ah (as in m*a*), *oh* (as in m*ow*), *oo* (as in m*oo*).

Step 3: Repetition
Select three different physical properties of an expressive action and
repeat this exploration several times.

Switching (Loves Me, Loves Me Not)

Explore the text "Loves me, loves me not." Each time you move from
"Loves me" to "loves me not" switch the physical property of the expressive action being explored. For example: "Loves me"—*fast*—
"loves me not"—*stable*, "Loves me"—*light*—"loves me not"—*heavy*.
Allow the physical properties of an expressive action to shift the manner in which you think and feel about the status of your love life. This
exercise can be quite playful and improvisatory.

Articulation Tongue Twister

Tongue-twister exercises are usually performed in a relatively fast and
charged manner in order to give all the moveable parts of the mouth
a thorough and comprehensive workout. However, these fast and
energized verbal drills often do nothing more than integrate the brain
and the mouth. The purpose here is to develop articulatory skills when

the body is in various physical states and, ideally, expressing a thought and a feeling.

Step 1
Select one of the following tongue twisters:

>Six sick slick slim sycamore saplings.
>A box of biscuits, a batch of mixed biscuits.
>Friendly Frank flips fine flapjacks.
>Vincent vowed vengeance very vehemently.
>Cheap ship trip.
>I cannot bear to see a bear.
>Mrs. Smith's Fish Sauce Shop.
>Knapsack straps.
>Lesser leather never weathered wetter weather better.
>Inchworms itching.
>A noisy noise annoys an oyster.
>The myth of Miss Muffet.
>Greek grapes.
>Moose noshing much mush.
>Which witch wished which wicked wish?
>The two-twenty-two train tore through the tunnel.
>Crisp crusts crackle crunchily.
>The Leith police dismisseth us.
>Ed had edited it.
>Quick kiss. Quicker kiss.

Step 2
Speak the tongue twister aloud multiple times, exploring each of the twenty physical properties of an expressive action.

Working with Dialogue I (Verbs)

Explore expressive action and language while working with a short scene.

Step 1

Select a verb from the verb list in the appendix for each phrase in the scene.

Step 2

Memorize the scene and explore it while playing the expressive actions you selected. Here's one example among many possibilities:

A: You don't have to explain anything. (*to block*)
B: No, listen, I need to . . . (*to drag up*)
A: Nor should you feel the need to explain anything. (*to gnaw*)
B: We are okay, right? (*to glaze over*)
A: Of course, we're okay. (*to hammer*)
B: I'm just not used to dealing with this. (*to fumble*)
A: No one is. (*to wonder*)
B: This is terrible. What have I done? (*to agonize*)
A: You really have screwed this one up. (*to promise*)
B: I will not accept it. I will not, I cannot, I won't! (*to lash out*)
A: What are you going to do about it, after the fact? (*to stand your ground*)
B: I will celebrate anyway. (*to boast*)
A: You can't be serious. (*to burn*)
(Shultz 2006)

Working with Dialogue II (Physical Properties)

Explore the physical properties of an expressive action while working with a short scene.

Step 1

Select a physical property of an expressive action for each phrase in the scene.

Step 2

Memorize the scene. Explore it while playing the physical property you selected. Here is one example among many possibilities:

A: Where have you been? (*sharp*)
B: Oh, you know me. Around. (*periphery*)
A: I can't believe that you're serious. (*direct*)

B: Well, I am. (*free*)

A: It just doesn't seem possible. (*diffused*)

B: If you think about it though . . . it really does make sense. (*slow*)

A: No, I get that. But the timing of everything makes it all the more . . . (*expansive*)

B: Farfetched? (*light*)

A: Implausible, but same difference. (*unstable*)

B: So what? (*contact*)

A: So, you're definitely going to do it? (*heavy*)

B: Absolutely. (*charged*)

A: I can't believe that this is happening. (*withdraw*)

B: Believe it. (*stable*)

A: How do you manage to always do this? (*release*)

B: Someone has to. (*bound*)

(Shultz 2006)

Working with Dialogue III (Monologue)

In the previous exercises, the lines were short and the expressive actions and language met in a simple and orderly line-by-line fashion. In the monologue below, you will have to make more complex choices about the manner in which expressive action integrates with the language of the text.

Consider the following interpretive choices:

■ Sometimes a simple sentence corresponds directly to the playing of one expressive action.

■ Sometimes multiple expressive actions are played in a single longer sentence.

■ Sometime expressive actions extend across two sentences or across several phrases (usually marked by a comma) within a sentence.

Step I
Read the monologue below aloud several times for meaning and content.

I've been wondering what we were talking about yesterday, and now everything seems perfectly clear to me. Because I keep talking and talking, and you get so tired of listening, you feel like your head will explode. Meanwhile, you've been really busy pretending I'm not here, and that you never met me and that we have no relationship at all. Sometimes when you're silent, not moving but just standing there still and distant, I come closer to you . . . so close . . . I become you and there is no me. When did you notice me? I mean really notice me. What did you see in me and how did you feel and where were your eyes? I'm your shadow. You move and I move with you. You feel me down your neck . . . even when I'm distant. I'm with you even when you're not here and you hate me for it.

Step 2
Explore the monologue on your feet. Read it aloud as you walk around the room. Each time you sense a shift in the thought and feeling of the character, walk in a different direction. Since a shift in thought and feeling represents a corresponding shift in expressive action, each time you change direction you will ultimately be asked to change the expressive action that you are playing.

Step 3
Based on your previous exploration, divide the language of the monologue into smaller phrases. The smaller phrases occur in places where you changed direction in Step 2.

Step 4
Select a verb from the verb list in the appendix, or select a physical property of an expressive action for each phrase of the monologue. Each smaller phrase should correspond directly to the playing of a single expressive action.

Step 5
Memorize the speech and explore it while playing the expressive actions you selected. Here is one example among many possiblities:

> I've been wondering what we were talking about yesterday, (*to gain control/bound*)

> and now everything seems perfectly clear to me. (*to forewarn/direct*)

> Because I keep talking and talking, and you get so tired of listening (*to harden/stable*) you feel like you head will explode. (*to recoil/withdraw*)

Meanwhile, you've been really busy pretending I'm not here, and that you never met me and that we have no relationship at all. (*to spiral out of control/unstable*)

Sometimes when you're silent, not moving but just standing there still and distant, I come closer to you . . . so close . . . I become you and there is no me. (*to haunt/light*)

When did you notice me? (*to badger/charged*)

I mean really notice me. (*to kick/fast*)

What did you see in me and how did you feel and where were your eyes? (*to aim/sharp*)

I'm your shadow. (*to apologize/release*)

You move and I move with you. (*to relinquish/heavy*)

You feel me down your neck . . . (*to affirm/slow*)

even when I'm distant. (*to reel back/contract*)

I'm with you even when you're not here and you hate me for it. (*to drone on/centered*)

Working with a Shakespearian Sonnet

In the sonnet below, you will have to make complex choices about the manner in which expressive action integrates with the language of the text and the metrical flow of the poetry.

Step 1
Read the sonnet below aloud several times for meaning, content, and metrical flow. The natural and consistent flow of the meter is like the pounding of your heart—in five simple beats (di-dum, di-dim, di-dum, di-dum, di-*dum*). The last *dum* of the line is given extra emphasis because it is the most important in the poetical pattern.

Sonnet 27

Weary with toil, I haste me to my *bed*,
The dear repose for limbs with travel *tired*,

But then begins a journey in my *head*
To work my mind, when body's work's *expired*;
For then my thoughts (from far where I *abide*)
Intend a zealous pilgrimage to *thee*,
And keep my drooping eyelids open *wide*,
Looking on darkness which the blind do *see*;
Save that my soul's imaginary *sight*
Presents [thy] shadow to my sightless *view*,
Which like a jewel hung in ghastly *night*,
Makes black night beauteous, and her old face *new*.
    Lo thus by day my limbs, by night my *mind*,
    For thee, and for myself, no quiet *find*.

Step 2

Explore the sonnet on your feet. Read the sonnet aloud as you walk around the room. Each time you sense a shift in the thought and feeling of the character, walk in a different direction. Since a shift in thought and feeling represents a corresponding shift in expressive action, each time you change direction you will ultimately be asked to change the expressive action that you are playing.

Step 3

Based on your previous exploration, divide the sonnet up into smaller phrases. The smaller phrases of the sonnet occur in places where you changed direction in Step 2.

Step 4

Select a verb from the verb list in the appendix, or select a physical property of an expressive action for each phrase of the sonnet. It is important to recognize that some of the best indications of expressive action are implicit in the language of the sonnet. Each smaller phrase should correspond directly to the playing of a single expressive action.

Step 5

Memorize the speech and explore it while playing the expressive actions you selected. (The last word of each line in the sonnet is printed in italics. This is to remind you, once again, that no matter how you choose to phrase the action of the sonnet, the iambic pentameter is driving you forward toward the end of each verse line. It is important to recognize that the most important rhyming words are placed at the end of the verse line.) Here is one example among many possibilities:

Sonnet 27

Weary with toil, (*to lament/heavy*)
I haste me to my *bed*, (*to luxuriate/light*)
The dear repose for limbs with travel *tired*, (*to stammer/indirect*)
But then begins a journey in my *head* (*to pound/heavy*)
To work my mind, (*to pound/fast*)
when body's work's *expired*; (*to expire/release*)
For then my thoughts (from far where I *abide*) (*to soar/expansive*)
Intend a zealous pilgrimage to *thee*, (*to soar charged*)
And keep my drooping eyelids open *wide*, (*to droop/heavy*)
Looking on darkness which the blind do *see*; (*to fumble/diffuse*)
Save that my soul's imaginary *sight* (*to race/light*)
Presents [thy] shadow to my sightless *view*, (*to race stable*)
Which like a jewel hung in ghastly *night*, (*to celebrate/charge*)
Makes black night beauteous, and her old face *new*. (*to contemplate/light*)
    Lo thus by day my limbs, by night my *mind*, (*to plod/unstable*)
    For thee, and for myself, no quiet *find*. (*to chagrin/sharp*)

Working on Your Own (Monologue and Scene Study)

Apply the principles explored above to a monologue or scene you are currently studying or would like to study. Remember that it isn't always necessary to find a verbal label for every expressive action in a scene. Many times expressive actions fall into place spontaneously and naturally. It is virtually impossible, misguided, and pedantic to find an intellectual label for every expressive action in a play. Use technique wisely and do not become a slave to it. Trust your impulses and your intuition. *Think* when you need to, and when it *feels* right it most often is right. What is most important is that you *know* or *sense* that you are playing a specific and exciting expressive action in each and every moment of the play. Whether you are intellectually aware of its verbal label is largely immaterial.

Contemporary Language Barre

Pair twenty pieces of text selected from twenty different contemporary plays with the twenty physical properties of an expressive action. (You will need to make interpretive choices about the language—structure, meaning, and intent—that is appropriate for the physical property selected.) Commit the barre to memory and repeat it as a part of your daily practice. In time, you may wish to change all or some of the texts for variety's sake.

Here's an example of a contemporary language barre:

- *Energy: charge.* BLANCHE: Why! I've been half crazy, Stella! When I found out you'd been insane enough to come back in here after what happened—I started to rush in after you! . . . What were you thinking of? Answer me! What? What? (*A Streetcar Named Desire*, Tennessee Williams)

- *Energy: release.* HAMM: It's the end of the day like any other day, isn't it Clov? (*Endgame*, Samuel Beckett)

- *Orientation: contact.* STANLEY: Mr. Whiteside, these gentlemen are deputy sheriffs. They have a warrant by which I am enabled to put you out of this house, and I need hardly add that it will be the greatest moment of my life Mr. Whiteside—. . . . I am giving you fifteen minutes in which to pack up and get out. If you are not gone in fifteen minutes, Mr. Whiteside, these gentlemen will forcibly eject you. (*The Man Who Came to Dinner*, George S. Kaufman and Moss Hart)

- *Orientation: withdraw.* CASY: I ain't preachin' no more much. The sperit ain't in the people no more; and worse'n that the sperit ain't in me no more. (*John Steinbeck's The Grapes of Wrath,* Frank Galati)

- *Size: expand.* MAGGIE: I tell you I got so nervous at that table tonight I thought I would throw back my head and utter a scream you could hear across the Arkansas border an' parts of Louisiana an' Tennessee. (*Cat on a Hot Tin Roof*, Tennessee Williams)

- *Size: contract.* SAMMY: I always worry that maybe people aren't going to like me, when I go to a party. Isn't that crazy? Do you ever get kind of a sick feeling in the pit of your stomach when you dread things? Gee, I wouldn't want to miss a party for anything. But every time I go to one, I have to reason with myself to keep from feeling that the whole world's against me. (*The Dark at the Top of the Stairs,* William Inge)

■ *Progression: center.* SISTER ALOYSIUS: I believe this man is creating or has already brought about an improper relationship with your son. (*Doubt: A Parable,* John Patrick Shanley)

■ *Progression: periphery.* EDNA: "The hills are alive with the sound of music" was the first best movie I ever saw and the first best music I ever heard. All I ever wanted to be in life was the star of that show. Someone who sang like a record and ran and twirled in the mountains. Someone so perfect that even the nuns couldn't understand her. Someone who said "Big Deal!" to the Germans and risked her life to save the sad children she was babysitting and then their gorgeous rich handsome father who thought his whole life was wrecked is now so happy and so thankful that he forgets all about his dead wife and then falls madly in love with me. (*The Good Times Are Killing Me*, Lynda Barry)

■ *Flow: free.* LINDA: We're free, We're free. (*Death of a Salesman*, Arthur Miller)

■ *Flow: bound.* HARPER: I WANT TO KNOW WHERE YOU'VE BEEN. I WANT TO KNOW WHAT'S GOING ON! (*Angels in America*, Tony Kushner)

■ *Direction: direct.* EMILY: I don't like the whole change that's come over you in the last year. I'm sorry if that hurts your feelings; but I've just got to—tell the truth and shame the devil . . . Well, up to a year ago, I used to like you a lot. And I used to watch you while you did everything—because we'd been friends so long. And then you began spending all your time at baseball. And you never stopped to speak to anybody anymore—not to really speak—not even to your own family you didn't. And George, it's a fact—ever since youve been elected captain, you've got awful stuch up and conceited, and all the girls say so. (*Our Town*, Thornton Wilder)

■ *Direction: indirect.* MARTHA: You know what's happened, George? You want to know what's *really happened*? It's snapped, finally. Not me . . . *it.* The whole arrangement. You can go along . . . forever, and everything's . . . manageable. You make all sorts of excuses to yourself . . . *you* know . . . this is life . . . the hell with it . . . maybe tomorrow he'll be dead . . . maybe tomorrow *you'll* be dead . . . all sorts of excuses. But then, one day, one night, something happens . . . and SNAP! It breaks. And you just don't give a damn anymore. I've tried with you, baby . . . really, I've tried. (*Who's Afraid of Virginia Woolf?* Edward Albee)

- *Speed: fast.* DAVE: He loved it, Martha! He ate it up! Get some! Get some a them gooks! Bap-bap-bap-bap-bap-bap! Blow'm away! (*Strange Snow*, Steve Metcalfe)

- *Speed: slow.* DR. CANTWAY: They were both my patients and they were two kids. I took care of both of them . . . of both their bodies. . . . And . . . for a brief moment I wondered if this is how God feels when he looks down at us. How we are all his kids . . . Our bodies . . . Our souls. . . . And I felt a great deal of compassion . . . for both of them. . . . (*The Laramie Project*, Moises Kaufman and the Tectonic Theater Project)

- *Weight: heavy.* RACHEL: At the funeral, Pa preached that Tommy didn't die in a state of grace, because his folks never had him baptized. (*Inherit the Wind*, Jerome Lawrence and Robert E. Lee)

- *Weight: light.* HOTCHKISS: How kind of you to say so, General! You're quite right: I am a snob. Why not? . . . I am a snob, not only in fact, but on principle. I shall go down in history, not as the first snob, but as the first avowed champion of English snobbery . . . (*Getting Married*, George Bernard Shaw)

- *Control: stable.* EDDIE: If you ain't a cowboy, you ain't shit. (*Fool for Love*, Sam Shepard [Altman film version])

- *Control: unstable.* EDMUND: Jesus, Papa, haven't you any pride or shame? And don't think I'll let you get away with it! I won't go to any damned state farm just to save you a few lousy dollars to buy more bum property with! You stinking old miser! (*Long Day's Journey into Night*, Eugene O'Neill)

- *Focus: sharp.* JOAN: What are you doing? Where are you going? What are you doing? You stay right there. Now. What were the two of you doing? I'm just asking a simple question. There's nothing to be ashamed of. (*Pause*) I can wait. (*Pause*) Were you playing "Doctor"? (*Sexual Perversity in Chicago*, David Mamet)

- *Focus: diffused.* BABE: Well, after I shot him, I put the gun down on the piano bench and then I went out into the kitchen and made up a pitcher of lemonade. . . . Yes, I was dying of thirst. My mouth was just as dry as a bone. . . . Right. I made it just the way I like it with lots of sugar and lots of lemon—about ten lemons in all. (*Crimes of the Heart*, Beth Henley)

Shakespearean Barre

Create a barre using speeches from Shakespeare's plays. Commit the barre to memory and repeat it as a part of your daily practice. In time, you may wish to change all or some of the texts for variety's sake. Here's an example:

- *Energy: charged.* HENRY V: Once more unto the breach, dear friends, once more; / Or close the wall up with our English dead. (*Henry V*, III.i)
- *Energy: released.* ROMEO: It is my lady, O, it is my love! (*Romeo and Juliet*, II.ii)
- *Orientation: contact.* MACBETH: Is this a dagger which I see before me, / The handle toward my hand? Come, let me clutch thee! (*Macbeth*, II.i)
- *Orientation: withdraw.* IAGO: For that I do suspect the lusty Moor / Hath leap'd into my seat; the thought whereof / Doth (like a poisonous mineral) gnaw my inwards; (*Othello*, II.i)
- *Size: expand.* CRESSIDA: Boldness comes to me now, and brings me heart. Prince Troilus, I have lov'd you night and day / For many weary months. (*Troilus and Cressida*, III.ii)
- *Size: contract.* DESDEMONA: I cannot say "whore." / It does abhor me now I speak the word; (*Othello*, IV.ii)
- *Progression: center.* CORDELIA: Good my Lord, / You have begot me, bred me, lov'd me: I / Return those duties back as are right fit, / Obey you, love you, and most honor you. (*King Lear*, I.i)
- *Progression: periphery.* SAMPSON: No, sir, I do not bite my thumb at you, sir, but I bite my thumb, sir. (*Romeo and Juliet,* I.i)
- *Flow: free.* PUCK: I go, I go, look how I go, / Swifter than an arrow from the Tartar's bow. (*A Midsummer Night's Dream*, III.ii)
- *Flow: bound.* CASSIO: Reputation, reputation, reputation! O, I have lost my reputation! I have lost the immortal part of myself, and what remains is bestial.—My reputation, Iago, my reputation! (*Othello*, II.iii)
- *Direction: direct.* CONSTANCE: Thou art [not] holy to belie me so, / I am not mad. This hair I tear is mine, / My name is Constance, I was Geffrey's wife, / Young Arthur is my son, and he is lost. / I am not mad, I would to heaven I were! (*King John*, III.iv)

- *Direction: indirect.* POLONIUS: Marry, well said, very well said. Look you, sir, / Inquire me first what Danskers are in Paris, / And how, and who, what means, and where they keep, / What company, at what expense; and finding / By this encompassment and drift of question / That they do know my son, (*Hamlet*, II.i)

- *Speed: fast.* JULIET: Gallop apace, you fiery-footed steeds, / Towards Phoebus' lodging; such a waggoner / As Phaëton would whip you to the west, / And bring in cloudy night immediately. (*Romeo and Juliet*, III.ii)

- *Speed: slow.* MACBETH: Tomorrow, and tomorrow, and tomorrow, / Creeps in this petty pace from day to day, / To the last syllable of recorded time; / And all our yesterdays have lighted fools / The way to dusty death. (*Macbeth*, V.v)

- *Weight: heavy.* HASTINGS: Woe, woe for England, not a whit for me! / For I, too fond, might have prevented this. (*Richard III*, III.iv)

- *Weight: light.* LUCENTIO: Tranio, I saw her coral lips to move, / And with her breath she did perfume the air. / Sacred and sweet was all I saw in her. (*The Taming of the Shrew*, I.i)

- *Control: stable.* LEONTES: Is whispering nothing? / Is leaning cheek to cheek? is meeting noses? / Kissing with inside lip? stopping the career / Of laughter with a sigh? (a note infallible / Of breaking honesty)? horsing foot on foot? / Skulking in corners? wishing clocks more swift? / Hours, minutes? noon, midnight? and all eyes / Blind with the pin and web but theirs, theirs only, / That would unseen be wicked? Is this nothing? (*The Winter's Tale*, I.ii)

- *Control: unstable.* GLOUCESTER: Thou sayest the King grows mad, I'll tell thee, friend, / I am almost mad myself. I had a son, / Now outlaw'd from my blood; he sought my life, / But lately, very late. I lov'd him, friend,— / Not father his son dearer; true to tell thee, / The grief hath craz'd my wits. (*King Lear*, III.iv)

- *Focus: sharp.* GLOUCESTER: Villains, set down the corse, or, by Saint Paul / I'll make a corse of him that disobeys. (*Richard III*, I.ii)

- *Focus: diffused.* BOTTOM: When my cue comes, call me, and I will answer. / My next is, "Most fair Pyramus." Heigh-ho! Peter Quince? / Flute the bellows-mender! Snout the tinker! Starveling! / God's my life, stol'n hence, and left me asleep! I have had / a most rare vision. I have had a dream, past the wit of man / to say what dream it was. (*A Midsummer's Night Dream*, IV.i)

Extended Language Barres

This exercise can be performed successfully only when either the contemporary or Shakespearean barre or both are fully memorized and can be repeated without interruption or prompting. Select one physical property for extended explorations. (See Chapter 15, pages 164–165, for details on what this entails.) Certain actions will change significantly, expressing new and different thoughts and feelings.

Expressive Action and Character

While it is commonly recognized that expressive action is essential to creating the authentic expression of feeling, its role in building a dramatic character is less understood. Expressive actions have a special transformative power that is often overlooked: they create character and personality. The personality of an individual can best be understood by examining their actions. *Who we are* is linked directly to *what we do*. We commonly identify character or personality with a series of adjectives—*rude, polite, aggressive, shy, funny*. However, character is not so much a trait a person possesses as an accumulation of consistent behavior revealed through action.

Suppose three separate drivers are pulled over by a police officer for speeding. The first attempts *to bicker* with the officer: "I was not going over the speed limit." The second attempts *to bluff* his way out of it: "Good evening, officer, was I doing anything wrong?" The third attempts *to beg* the officer for mercy: "But you just can't give me a ticket. You just can't." The three speeding drivers have three distinct personalities, which are demonstrated in the different expressive actions they play. Their expressive actions trigger our understanding of their character and their personality.

Each of these expressive actions—*to bicker, to bluff,* and *to beg*—could be described in less active terms. The bickering speeder could be called *aggressive*; the bluffing speeder, *slick*; and the begging speeder, a *victim*. However, none of these static descriptions provide the actor with anything specific *to do*. It is not that an actor should never think of a character in static terms. This may be a very useful part of the intellectual and interpretive process. However, until these intellectual ideas about the character reveal or manifest themselves in playable expressive actions, they have little power. The personality of the character being played is communicated most directly through a series of structured and selective expressive actions.

Body structure—defined in Chapter 4 as "the way we shape ourselves or have been shaped by our life experience"—contributes to an even more detailed understanding of personality and character. Body structures are characterized by modes of expression that are:

1. consistently used over time,
2. automatic or involuntary, and
3. can be modified only through conscious effort.

To some extent, we all have a somewhat fixed body structure—a habitual way we like to structure and organize our actions and behavior. Consequently, a person's body structure shapes and influences self-expression, character, and personality.

The concept of body structure suggests that character and personality are not simply psychological patterns occurring in the brain but physical patterns living and residing in our bodies. Character, in many ways, is a type of limitation—a habitual manner and method of behaving and moving. A clinically depressed person has a different body structure from that of a paranoid schizophrenic. A light-hearted, easygoing, happy-go-lucky person has a different body structure from that of a stern, straight-laced, mild-mannered person. When playing a character in a play, an actor has to make certain choices about the physical patterns that the character uses to express thought and feeling. This, of course, involves a thorough analysis of the script, but it also requires a type of physical research. Ideally, the actor selects a series of expressive actions that appropriately reflect these limitations.

For example, you could determine that a character like Blanche DuBois in *A Streetcar Named Desire* has a propensity to play *indirect, light, free,* and *peripheral* expressive actions and a character like Medea in *Medea* has a propensity to play *direct, charged, stable,* and *heavy* expressive actions. It can be useful to think of character as a type of computer font (see Figure 16.1). Just as these two fonts influence and shape the manner and method in which the words appear on the page, the physical properties of an expressive action influence and shape the character.

The following exercises help you use specific physical properties characteristic of an expressive action to build a consistent and believable character. Remember that while characters do behave in

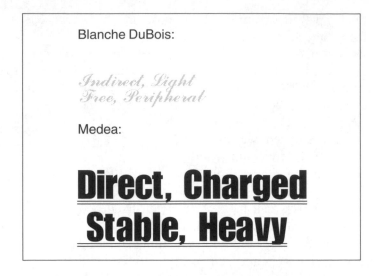

Figure 16.1 Character

consistent and predictable ways in plays, they also grow, change, and evolve, and sometimes behave erratically and unpredictably. Ultimately, all the actor's physical work on character must be rooted in a thorough understanding of the script.

Perform a Physical Task

Build three different characters by exploring three physical properties of an expressive action. (Spend some time improvising before settling on the parameters of your specific character study.)

Step 1: Prompt
- Character 1: *fast, contact, stable*
- Character 2: *direct, bound, slow*
- Character 3: *heavy, unstable, center*

Step 2: Basic Exercise
Complete the following physical activity as you explore the physical properties of each of the three characters.

1. Open door.
2. Enter room.
3. Close door.
4. Call out, "Is anybody home?"
5. Discover that no one else is home.
6. Cross to counter.
7. Set down groceries.
8. Take off coat.
9. Cross to chair.
10. Place coat on back of chair.
11. Return to counter.
12. Start to unpack groceries.
13. Find something to eat in the grocery bag.
14. Find newspaper in the grocery bag.
15. Cross to chair and table.
16. Read and eat.

To help you in these character studies, ask two essential questions:

1. *Are the three physical properties of an expressive action fully integrated in the body as you perform the physical task?* If you feel you are consciously focusing on moving slowly, stably, or directly, for example, the physical properties have probably not been fully integrated in your body.

2. *Do you feel you're a different person?* This is a subjective question, but useful nevertheless. Character transformation is successful when you feel you are moving and behaving as if you are somebody else. This can only be determined by felt experience. It may help to compare the feeling or sensation of a character in the body to different types of perfume. Just as different perfumes smell different, your three different characters should feel different.

"Being Brilliant"

Using the three physical properties selected for each of the three characters above, prepare the monologue below three times, as each of the three characters you have developed:

Would you like to be brilliant? Not just . . . I don't mean just "out-standing." I mean the sort of thing that would separate you, really separate you from others. Just: Would you like to be brilliant? a reservoir? a flood? With a kind of light inside you that other people . . . do you know what I am saying? found hard to look at—see, understand. Like a certain pain. Like fire. Brilliant. Even if it meant . . . well, alone: being alone. More than graceful. More than funny. More than very good, competent. Like fire. Like light on snow. Brilliant. So intense that . . . I mean really: don't you think we slow ourselves down for other people? Haven't you ever thought that? What if either of us, you or I, never stopped ourselves, never slowed ourselves, allowed resistance? Can you imagine the light, the velocity we might . . . I want to be brilliant—at least one thing. Don't you want that too? Don't you think you could be? Don't you think you could startle something in the world? I want to be amazing; I think you could be amazing. I am trying, please, to think about things. That's all. I am trying to think. I see things happening. I see a door-way. I'm at a door. Ready to walk in or out of . . . some house. You see: I see things getting very . . . choices. Yes. We are talking choices. And I'm not settling. (Kranes)

To help you, ask two essential questions:

1. *Are the three physical properties of an expressive action fully integrated in your body as you perform the monologue?* If you feel you are consciously talking in a bound, charged, or indirect way, for example, the physical properties have probably not been fully integrated with the language.
2. *Do you feel you're a different person?*

Epilogue
Artistic Expression and Aesthetics

Most actor training programs are committed to training actors for what they nobly refer to as the *professional theatre*. In addition to offering acting, voice, movement, and play-reading classes, a great deal of time is also spent sharing the secrets of *show business*. The students learn all about résumés, headshots, casting calls, agents, unions, and how to survive in New York, Los Angeles, or Chicago. Many maintain this "business" training is essential and all-important, as if the commerce of theater were a complicated and sophisticated subject.

In fact, theatre is a surprisingly simple business, especially compared to computer technology, pharmaceuticals, aerospace, the stock market, or the insurance trade. Because of recent advances in technology, other industries have experienced profound and revolutionary changes, while the business of acting has remained relatively unchanged for centuries. Most of what the ambitious and determined actor needs to know about the commerce of theatre can be gleaned from reading any one of several very good books currently available on the subject.

While teaching students that theatre is a business is widely accepted, teaching them that it is an art is too often ignored. Too little time is spent preparing actors to be artists or even talking about the function and purpose of art. This short chapter is in no way an exhaustive study of the actor's art. It is a primer that I hope will answer some important questions, challenge some old ideas, and most important, stimulate more discussion on this much-neglected subject.

Science and Art

Articulating the purpose and function of art is a tricky business. Nonetheless, a preliminary understanding of *art* can be gained by distinguishing it from its complement, *science*. *Art* refers to the creative contribution of poets, musicians, dancers, actors, novelists, painters, and so on. *Science* in its broadest sense refers to any systematized or structured method of knowing—not only the natural sciences (biology, chemistry, and physics) but also the social sciences (sociology, psychology, anthropology, even history).

Science and art provide two different perspectives of our world. Science seeks to develop our intellectual appreciation for how the world works. Art, on the other hand, seeks to develop our appreciation for sensory experience. When our senses are educated, our understanding of emotion and feeling is simultaneously strengthened and enhanced. Developing sensitivity to human feeling is a central aim of almost all artistic creation.

Most individuals have a great appreciation for the purpose and importance of science. However, they are hard pressed to articulate an intelligent or remotely compelling justification for the purpose or importance of art. When pressed they invariably resort to the need for entertainment or escape. It has never occurred to them that art is responsible for feeding and developing the spirit in the same way that science feeds and develops the mind. Science in America thrives and is well funded, while art programs falter, underfunded and underattended. Unfortunately, Western culture has traditionally rewarded thinking and devalued sensing and feeling.

At the university in which I teach, undergraduate students are required to take one course in the fine arts and six in the sciences. When a moment is set aside to teach art, the senses are rarely educated. In most classrooms in this country, art is taught like a science. Scientific methods of identification and classification are applied indiscriminately to the study of art, music, poetry, theatre, and dance. Students spend hours memorizing dates, movements, titles, historical perspectives, and biographical data. Students are taught *to think* about works of art but not *to feel* them. Rarely are the subjective aspects of viewing a painting, listening to music, or watching a play celebrated or encouraged.

A balanced world requires individuals balanced in thinking and feeling to people it. In the last century, the attention and celebration of the sciences has been greater and more profound than at any time in our history. Each new scientific discovery poses a new set of ethical and moral questions that present tough choices that have serious consequences. What do we do with our nuclear waste? Should we genetically alter our food? Do we want to know if we have the gene for

Alzheimer's disease? It is not simply enough to have the technology to do these extraordinary things; we must also know how we *feel* about doing these extraordinary things. These questions have no rational, logical, scientific answers. They are human questions. The answers are intuitive, a product of felt experience, requiring a logic of the spirit and a wisdom of the heart.

The world's most complicated ethical, moral, and spiritual issues are explored in great works of art. All the while a great work of art is entertaining us and providing us with pleasure, it is subtly and indirectly preparing us to answer complicated moral and ethical questions. Most of the lay population's ethical and moral education about the intellectual advances of the world's leading scientists and thinkers comes from popular films, television, novels, and plays. Genetics, disease, history, women's rights, racism, homosexuality, space travel, environmental issues, and so on all receive a thorough and important human treatment in art. Art puts science in a palatable wrapper so that even those unschooled in the ways of scientific thought can grapple with complex human issues.

Art explores the sciences from a human perspective. Popular movies like *Jurassic Park* explain to the nonscientific world the dangers of mixing genetic engineering and theme park entertainment. Ibsen taught his generation the important role heredity and environment play in determining human destiny. Generations have learned more about English history from the plays of Shakespeare than from any history book. Jerome Lawrence and Robert E. Lee challenged the nation to examine evolution—a tough issue at the time and again today—in their dramatic exploration of the Scopes "monkey" trial, in the play *Inherit the Wind*.

Science is the objective study of serious subjects. Art is the subjective study of serious subjects. Scientists and artists are equally important. A culture with strong science and strong art has nothing to fear from its technological advances. A culture with strong science and weak art has everything to fear.

A socialist and a capitalist go to a production of *Death of a Salesman*. Afterward, they have an intellectual discussion about the play. The socialist views Willy Loman as a victim of capitalism, free enterprise, profit, and a false American dream. The capitalist views him as a lazy, unethical liar—a silly dreamer and a blowhard who would rather talk than work. The capitalist and socialist have very different intellectual ideas about the play. However, putting their intellectual ideas aside and discussing the way the play made them feel, both the socialist and capitalist acknowledge that they were moved by a sense of compassion for the desperate, lonely, and isolated Willy Loman. Perhaps this common compassion can pave the way for them to synthesize their seemingly irreconcilable philosophical differences.

What is most important about good theatre is not the differing thoughts, interpretations, and intellectual biases we bring to it but its power to unite every observer emotionally and even spiritually. To truly understand theatre—or any work of art—we must turn our discussion away from what we think and begin to discuss how the work of art makes us feel. Ultimately, a work of art cannot be appreciated in light of the intellectual baggage that we bring to it but in light of its direct appeal to our feelings. Most important, what a work of art makes us feel can sometimes change the way we think. This is art's greatest and most profound achievement.

Significant Form

The actor, like all artists, is a *form maker*. Painters create visual forms by arranging pigment on canvas. Musicians organize pitch and rhythm into musical forms recognizable as melody. Dancers organize shifts of weight into the physical form of a dance. Actors organize the voice and body into meaningful forms of expression that reveal the life of the character they are portraying. A work of art, like many other things, can be either *significant* or *insignificant*. When the artistic creation is well done, the work of art possesses *significant form*.

Significant forms are intense, appealing, commanding, and profound. Any time that we are captivated in the theater, struck by a painting, or moved by a piece of music, we have encountered significant form. Aesthetic philosopher Susanne K. Langer (1953) defines significant form "as the essence of everything artful. It is what is meant by anything we call artistic."

The creation of significant form is primarily a product of selection, of conscious and unconscious choices by the artist. A work of art achieves significance when the raw materials of the artist's craft are organized and structured in a skillful and meaningful way. The painter selects paint, color, brushes, brush strokes, and a canvas; the musician selects the appropriate key, time signature, and musical notes; the dancer selects a sequence of rhythmically organized weight shifts and gestures; and the actor selects a unified series of expressive actions that reveal the life of the character.

It is difficult to describe in words what makes a work of art significant. Before the advent of modern art, all significant art was simply called *beautiful*. Art was considered a study of the beautiful and the art objects created were also beautiful. Though the term *beautiful* is applied less frequently to contemporary works of art, the concept of beauty is central to an understanding of significant form. Human beings possess an extraordinary aesthetic appreciation for the beautiful. Our fascination with mountains, fireworks, flowers, children, starry nights, rainbows, and sunsets all reflect a celebration of the beautiful. Painted houses, furniture groupings, fashion, gardens, parks, makeup, jewelry, and hairstyles demonstrate the human creature's seemingly illogical need to perpetuate the beautiful. The fine arts—music, dance, painting, poetry, and theatre—are codified aesthetic extensions of this obsession with the beautiful.

In the twentieth century, insightful artists began to find new subjects of beauty in unfamiliar places; the term *beautiful* became inappropriate and fell out of fashion. It is hard, in the traditional sense, to describe *Waiting for Godot*, *No Exit*, or *Marat Sade* as beautiful. Indeed, much of modern and postmodern art, while possessing a unique and special appeal, seems to defy the traditional beautiful label. When the term *beautiful* failed to satisfy, it was difficult to find new language that could adequately describe the import of modern art. Some art critics avoided the problem altogether and simply asserted that the import of great art was beyond description. Others sought to create new terms.

The seemingly ambiguous term *suchness and otherness* is a fine example of this new terminology. A work of art is said to possess *suchness and otherness* when its import is so great that the spectator is convinced its brilliance and depth is something other than and like no such thing experienced before. Art objects with *suchness and otherness* undoubtedly possess significant form. Similarly, scholar and philosopher F. S. C. Northrop (1962) replaced the imprecise and seemingly inappropriate term *beautiful* with *radical, empirical immediacy*. It took Northrop three very erudite words, and undoubtedly a great deal of sound thinking, to articulate precisely what makes a work of art significant. Nonetheless, Northrop's *radical, empirical immediacy* is aptly coined. Significant art is *radical*, possessing boldness—a rebellious and revolutionary quality. *Empirical* suggests a direct appeal to the senses. A significant work of art is a celebration—an exploitation of and some-times an assault on the senses. *Immediacy* refers to the commanding presence of a well-constructed work of art. Significant art attracts, invites, and demands attention. While any term attempting to articu-late what makes a work of art great may fail to satisfy, the terms *suchness and otherness* and *radical, empirical immediacy* are very useful in clari-fying what makes a work of art significant.

As we begin this new century, acting in America would benefit greatly from a responsible discussion of the importance of significant form. The legacy of Stanislavski in America has resulted in an unprec-edented call for *truthfulness* and *honesty*—a type of everyday realism, a slice of life. Actors practice emotional substitution, create volumi-nous life biographies for the characters they play, personalize and ask, "What would I do if I were in this situation?"—all in search of a hon-est and truthful performance.

Though this quest for truthfulness was well intended and useful, the effort was not without its shortcomings. In some circles a *naively realistic* approach to acting has emerged, rendering style destructive, heightened language unnatural, largesse of expression taboo, voice and movement training inessential, and character transformation unnec-essary. Absurdly, actors are encouraged to simply be themselves.

Certainly, the actor's work must be truthful, plausible, and most important authentic, but beyond that it must be exciting, vital, and dynamic. What is commonly rewarded in many acting circles as *truth-ful* and *honest* work is often pedestrian, mundane, and sometimes even boring. Not everything that is truthful is necessarily artful. If it were, there would be art all around us. Rarely—and perhaps thankfully—is everyday life exciting, structured, or stylized enough to be worthy of the label theatrical, significant, or artful. A mature discussion of acting requires that we move beyond truth and believability and also include in our aesthetic criteria a newfound appreciation for signifi-cant form. The actor's primary responsibility is not merely to live truth-fully in imaginary circumstances but also to live artfully in imaginary circumstances.

Living Form

The problem for the actor, and all artists, is that terms like *truthful, believable,* and *honest* are ambiguous. What is truthful to one person may or may not be truthful to others. The terms are subjective and provide actors with little objective information about the quality of their performance or how to improve it.

Most responsible actors desire some practical and experiential understanding of what it means to be truthful, believable, and honest. These terms suggest quite simply that the performance of the actor is lifelike, alive, living—that it exhibits the discernable physical properties of what Susanne K. Langer (1957) calls *living form*. An actor exhibiting living form appears to grow, change, and evolve naturally and organically, as all living creatures do. The actor's body is not rigid and mechanical but rather flexible, adaptable, and resourceful. An actor whose performance exhibits the properties of living form expands and contracts, charges and releases, contacts and withdraws, doing so with vitality, integrity, and authenticity. The flow of the body is free, uninterrupted, and fluid. The progression of movement begins deep within the center of the body and expands sequentially into the legs, arms, hands, feet, and head. The action, regardless of how small or subtle, is comprehensive and full-bodied. Each movement is harmonic and rhythmic, punctuated by a clearly differentiated beginning, middle, and end. Most important, the concept of living form makes explicit that truthful acting is not just a product of some type of intangible inner commitment or mental affirmation but simultaneously a richly structured physical experience.

Real and Imaginary Feelings

The type of feeling experienced by the actor is of a different kind and nature than the type of feeling experienced in daily life. These two distinct types of feelings are identified by various terms: *psychological feeling* and *aesthetic feeling*, *subjective feelings* and *objective feelings*, *imaginary feelings* and *real feelings*. Regardless of the terminology, the assertion is that there is a distinction between the type of emotional experience present in daily life and the kind of emotional experience present in a work of art (Hornby 1992). Some art critics go so far as to suggest that the feelings experienced when viewing a work of art are not so much one's own personal feelings but rather the feelings that belong to the art object itself. A significant work of art, when viewed without personal entanglement, arouses feelings that are uniquely its own.

In saying this, I have probably offended many readers, who will have rushed to the conclusion that I am suggesting that acting is merely artifice and technical demonstration: "Acting must be real." "I am my character." "I only draw on my personal experiences." Suggesting that the actor experiences a special type of feeling is in no way meant to diminish or lessen its importance. A great deal of sound thinking suggests that there is a special type of feeling reserved solely for artistic expression.

You and a friend go to see a movie. You are both emotionally moved by the movie and leave the theatre with tears running down your faces. On your way out of the theatre, you encounter another friend who is going to see the next showing. He asks, "How was the movie?" You respond, "Wonderful! Wonderful! It was one of the best movies I ever saw." Your weeping friend, on the other hand, says nothing and hurries toward the car. On the way home, your friend is especially quiet. To break the silence you ask, "Did you like the movie?" She responds by stating that she does not want to talk about it.

The most important distinction between you and your friend's experiences is one of perspective. Your imaginative feelings allowed you to experience the movie. Her real feelings interrupted and distorted her perceptions of the movie. Perhaps it closely mirrored a personal problem she was currently experiencing, reminded her of a traumatic childhood experience, or even evoked new concerns or fears of which she was previously unaware. Your friend did not experience the imaginative world of the film, because she was caught up in the drama of her own life. If asked about the film, it is doubtful whether she could provide any objective response at all. Of course, you must not diminish the importance of your imaginary feelings simply because they were different from your friend's. The tears streaming down your face during the movie were quite real. They were powerful and authentic. However, they had no real bearing on the outcome, course, or direction of your life. You could feel them completely and freely without consequence or fear. Because you were able to make an aesthetic distinction between your real life and the pretend life of the movie, you were able to enjoy these feelings, no matter how sad, horrible, or depressing they might have been, and learn from them.

If we put aside all the romantic talk about the necessary emotional turmoil of the truly committed actor, we should agree—at least on some level—that there is a difference between our real feelings and those of the characters we play. The stereotypical method actor with his illicit personalization and compulsive quest for real feeling may have created an emotional response that interferes with or blocks the feelings contained in the play itself. A very wise instructor of mine

would frequently comment, "I wasn't aware the play was about you."
I have never forgotten this cryptic statement. It was meant to challenge
the imagination.

A Practical Handbook for the Actor (Burder et al. 1986) states, "The
actor's job is not to bring the truth of his personal experience to the
stage, but rather to bring the truth of himself to the specific needs of
the plays." Susanne K. Langer (1953) goes so far as to suggest that the
truth the artist may be seeking may transcend the self:

> [T]he artist need not have experienced in actual life every emotion
> he can express. It may be through manipulation of his created ele-
> ments that he discovers new possibilities of feeling, strange moods,
> perhaps greater concentration of passion than his old temperament
> could ever produce or his fortunes have yet to call forth. (374)

The job of the actor is not to reduce the complexity of the character to
the confines of limited personal experience but rather to allow the character to expand the actor's own human potential. The problem with real
feelings is that they are subjective. When an actor's real feelings are
substituted for those of the character being played, the play becomes
muddied and distorted. Just like your friend who could not objectively
experience the movie, actors who are overcome with their personal
feelings often lose all objectivity about the quality of their performance.
Real feelings are difficult to shape and focus into meaningful and significant form. They are usually beyond control. The mistake is to assume
that because real feelings are powerful and truly felt they are artistically
satisfying for the audience. When an actor is entangled in personal feelings, the audience members are often duped into paying more attention
to the actor than to the character being portrayed or to the play. Some
actors, unfortunately, have reduced some of the theatre's greatest plays
to a petty exploration of whatever trivial personal entanglement happens to be occurring in their own lives. When great actors build great
characters, they are undoubtedly drawing upon their past personal experiences, not for the purposes of finding real feelings, but for a deeper
understanding of their imaginary ones. The best acting is not a valida-
tion of one's own life but transcendence into a larger and deeper understanding of the human condition.

Smart actors with emotional stability and longevity recognize that
all the world is not a stage. The actor's personal life is not the theatrical equivalent of the dancer's ballet barre and the violinist's musical
scales. Fortunately, the talented actor can transcend, through strong

technique and a powerful imagination, any personal limitation and embrace any character or experience conjured up by even the most inventive playwright.

The distinction between imaginary and real feelings is not always as apparent in practice as it is in theory. Distinguishing real and imaginary feeling is not meant to deny that in the process of training or in rehearsals imaginary feelings can revert to or become confused with real feelings. The fine line between real and imaginary feeling can easily become blurred or disappear altogether. Just as it is possible to view a movie that hits too close to home, it is possible to stumble onto imaginary feelings in rehearsal that cannot be disassociated from real ones. This is often the case, particularly in the initial stages of the actor's development, when the necessary sophistication to navigate the emotional instrument has not yet been developed. The occasional confusion of real and imaginary feeling is a part of the process of learning and a hazard of the profession. Even the most skilled actors can on occasion find themselves in real emotional trouble. What is important and necessary is that the actor, the director, the other actors, or the acting teacher recognize that the imaginary process has reverted to a real one and that responsible and conscious choices be made about how to proceed. Actors are always dancing a fine line between the real and the imaginary.

Pure Form

When an actor's technique rises to the level of sophistication where personal feelings are not confused or muddled with those of the character, an extraordinary thing takes place. The actor, without recourse to personal limitations, is able to tap into and unlock the pure form of human feeling. Pure form is a highly specialized type of feeling that requires a selflessness and "egolessness" rarely exhibited in Western acting. The Hindus identified this highest type of metaphysical feeling as *rasa*:

> This last they call *rasa*; it is a state of emotional knowledge, which comes only to those who have long studied and contemplated poetry. It is supposed to be of supernatural origin, because it is not like mundane feeling and emotion, but is detached, more of the spirit than of the viscera, pure and uplifting. *Rasa* is, indeed, that compre-

hension of the directly experienced "inward" life that all art conveys. (Langer 1953, 323)

Rasa is the Hindu understanding of pure form. Pure form occurs when the actor becomes selfless. Ironically, the deepest and most profound expression of feeling occurs not through getting into the self but by transcending the self. Ultimately, pure form provides the actor with a boundless and limitless range of expression. This egoless and selfless form of expression cannot occur without technique. All good technique, through the process of repetition, discipline, and dedication, results in a type of self-cleansing and self-transcendence that triumphs over personal limitations, obstacles, inexperience, and idiosyncrasies. Good technique puts the actor in touch with the perfect self.

Yoshi Oida, the famous Japanese actor, in his own way touches on pure form and the egoless actor in his book *The Invisible Actor* (1997):

> For me, acting is not about showing my presence or displaying my technique. Rather it is about revealing, through acting, 'something else,' something that the audience does not encounter in daily life. . . . For this to happen, the audience must not have the slightest awareness what the actor is doing. They must be able to forget the actor. The actor must disappear. In Kabuki theatre, there is a gesture, which indicates 'looking at the moon,' where the actor points into the sky with his index finger. One actor who was very talented performed this gesture with grace and elegance. The audience thought: 'Oh, his movement is so beautiful!' They enjoyed the beauty of his performance and the technical mastery he displayed. Another actor made the same gesture, pointing at the moon. The audience didn't know whether or not he moved elegantly; they simply saw the moon. I prefer this kind of actor: the one who shows the moon to the audience. The actor who can become invisible. (xvii–xviii)

When the actor's expression finds pure form, its impact has a consistent and universal appeal. All in the audience observe with clarity and complete human understanding the same unselfish, archetypal human truth. Something great is attained when an actor moves beyond mundane and muddied everyday feelings and embraces without resistance the pure form of feeling. We see feeling with a greater precision than ever possible in the context of daily living. This selfless rendering of pure form is at the heart of the emotional education of the actor, the audience, and our culture.

Appendix
Verb List

Below is an exhaustive list of verbs that may be used as prompts for expressive action. The list may be more comprehensive than practical, and some may assert that many of the actions listed are virtually unplayable. However, it is meant to spark the imagination of the actor rather than curtail it. Surprisingly many gifted actors select the seemingly most difficult or unlikely of verbs and organize them into meaningful and productive expressive actions.

A

to abandon
to abduct
to abhor
to abide
to abolish
to absorb
to abuse
to ace
to accelerate
to accept
to access
to acclaim
to accommodate
to accost
to address
to adhere
to admit
to admire
to admonish
to adopt
to adore
to adorn
to advance

to advert
to advise
to advocate
to afflict
to affirm
to aggravate
to agonize
to agitate
to agree
to aid
to aim
to alarm
to alert
to alienate
to align
to allocate
to allot
to allow
to allude
to allure
to ally
to amaze
to amble
to amuse

to angle for
to announce
to anoint
to annoy
to annihilate
to antagonize
to anticipate
to answer
to apologize
to appeal
to appraise
to approach
to approve
to arbitrate
to argue
to arm
to arouse
to arrange
to ascertain
to ask
to aspire
to assail
to assent
to assess

to assign
to assist
to assure
to atone
to attest
to attract
to audition
to avenge
to awaken
to award

B

to back away
to back down
to back off
to back out
to back up
to bail
to balance
to balk
to ban
to bandy about
to banish
to bank on
to bar from
to bargain
to barge in
to bark
to barrel along
to barter
to bask
to bat around
to batten down
to battle
to bawl out
to bay
to beam
to bear
to bear down
to bear out
to beat
to beat about
to beat down

to beat up
to beckon
to beef up
to beg
to beguile
to bequeath
to beset
to besiege
to besmirch
to bestow
to bet
to bias
to bicker
to bellow
to bind down
to bitch
to bite
to blab
to blame
to blank out
to blanket
to blast
to bless
to blitz
to block
to blossom
to blot out
to blow up
to bluff
to blurt out
to blush
to boast
to boil
to bolt
to bomb
to bombard
to bone up
to boogie down
to book up
to boost
to boot
to booze it up
to borrow

to boss
to bother
to bottle up
to bounce
to bow out
to bow down
to bowl over
to box in
to brace up
to brace for
to brag
to brainwash
to brave out
to break
to break away
to break through
to break up
to break down
to breeze along
to breeze in
to breeze through
to bribe
to brief
to brighten up
to brim over
to bring about
to bring around
to bring into line
to bring out
to bring up
to bristle
to broach
to brush aside
to brush away
to brush off
to brush up
to bubble over
to bubble up
to buck for
to buckle down
to bulldoze
to bully
to bum around

to bum out
to bumble
to bump
to bump along
to bunch
to bundle
to bungle up
to burden
to burn
to burst
to bury
to bust out
to bust up
to bustle
to butt in
to butt out
to butter up
to button one's lip
to buzz along
to buzz off

C
to cage
to cajole
to calculate
to call
to call down
to campaign
to cancel
to capitalize
to capitulate
to care about
to care for
to carp
to carry on
to carve out
to cast aside
to cast away
to cast down
to cast off
to catch off guard
to cater
to caution

to cave in
to celebrate
to cement
to censure
to center on
to challenge
to change
to channel
to charge
to charm
to chart out
to chase after
to chase away
to chat
to chatter
to cheat
to check
to check out
to check over
to cheer
to chew out
to chew over
to chicken out
to chide
to chill out
to chime in
to chip away
to chisel
to choke
to choose
to chop
to chortle
to chow down
to chuck away
to chuckle
to chug along
to chum up
to churn out
to circle
to cite
to claim
to clam up
to clamor

to clamp down
to clash
to clasp
to claw
to clear
to cleave
to click
to climb
to cling
to clip
to cloak
to clock
to clog
to close
to closet
to cloud
to clown
to clue in
to clunk
to cluster
to clutch
to clutter
to coach
to coalesce
to coast along
to coax
to coerce
to coil
to collaborate
to collapse
to collect
to collide
to collude
to come around
to come at someone
to come between
to come clean
to come down on
to come over
to come through
to commend
to comment
to commiserate

to commit
to commune
to communicate
to commute
to compare
to compel
to compensate
to compete
to compile
to complain
to compliment
to comply
to compress
to compromise
to compute
to con
to conceal
to concede
to conceive
to concentrate
to concern
to condemn
to confer
to confess
to confide
to confine
to confirm
to confiscate
to conflict
to conform
to confront
to confuse
to congratulate
to conjure
to connect
to connive
to consecrate
to consent
to consider
to console
to consort
to conspire
to constrain

to construct
to construe
to consult
to contend
to convalesce
to converge
to converse
to convert
to convey
to convict
to convince
to cook up
to cool down
to cool off
to cooperate
to coordinate
to cop out
to cope
to cork up
to correspond
to cough up
to counsel
to cover
to cover up
to cower
to cozy up
to crack down
to crack up
to cram
to crash
to crave
to crawl
to creep
to cringe
to criticize
to cross
to crouch
to crow
to crowd
to crown
to cruise
to crumple
to crunch

to crusade
to crush
to cry
to cuddle
to cue in
to curse
to cuss out
to cut
to cut down

D

to dab
to dabble
to dally
to damn
to dance
to dangle
to dart
to dash
to dawn upon
to daydream
to deal
to debate
to deceive
to decide
to deck out
to declare
to decorate
to dedicate
to deduce
to deduct
to deface
to default
to defect
to defend
to defer
to define
to deflect
to defraud
to deign
to delegate
to deliberate
to delight

to deliver
to delude
to deluge
to delve
to demand
to demonstrate
to demote
to denounce
to dent
to deny
to depart
to depend
to deposit
to deprive
to descend
to describe
to desert
to design
to designate
to despair
to despise
to detach
to detect
to deter
to detract
to develop
to deviate
to devote
to dicker
to dictate
to diddle
to die
to differ
to differentiate
to diffuse
to dig
to dig down
to digress
to dilly-dally
to dip
to direct
to disagree
to discipline

to disclose
to disconnect
to discourage
to discriminate
to discuss
to disembark
to disengage
to disentangle
to disguise
to disgust
to dismiss
to dispatch
to display
to dispose
to dispute
to disqualify
to dissociate
to dissolve
to dissuade
to distance
to distinguish
to distract
to dive
to diverge
to divide
to divorce
to divulge
to divvy
to dodder
to dodge
to dole out
to doll up
to doom
to dose
to doss
to dote
to draft
to drag
to drag down
to drag up
to drain
to drape
to draw apart

to draw out
to draw together
to dream
to dredge
to drift
to drill
to drip
to drive
to drive out
to drone
to drop
to drown
to drown out
to drum
to duke out
to dwell on

E
to ease
to eavesdrop
to edge around
to egg on
to eke out
to elaborate
to elbow
to embellish
to emblazon
to embroil
to empathize
to empower
to enable
to encourage
to endeavor
to enforce
to engage
to enlighten
to enlist
to enshrine
to ensnare
to entangle
to entertain
to enthrall
to entice

to entrap
to entreat
to entrust
to envision
to envy
to erase
to erupt
to escape
to escort
to establish
to estimate
to evict
to exact
to examine
to exceed
to excite
to exclude
to excuse
to exhort
to exile
to exonerate
to exorcise
to expand
to expect
to expel
to expend
to experiment
to explain
to explode
to expostulate
to express
to extend
to extol
to extort
to exult

F

to face
to fade
to fail
to faint
to fake
to fall

to fall apart
to fall in love
to fall into a trap
to falter
to familiarize
to fan out
to fancy
to fashion
to fault
to favor
to fawn over
to fear
to feel out
to fence in
to fend for
to fess up
to feud
to fiddle
to fidget
to fight
to figure on
to find out
to finish
to fink on
to fink out
to fire at
to fish
to fix up
to fizzle out
to flag down
to flake out
to flame up
to flap
to flare
to flash
to flatten
to flee
to flick
to flicker
to flinch
to fling
to float
to flog

to flood
to flop
to flounce
to flow
to flow over
to flub
to fluctuate
to fluff
to flunk
to flush
to flutter
to fly
to foam
to focus
to fog up
to foist
to fold
to follow
to fool around
to force
to forewarn
to forgive
to fortify
to foul up
to fraternize
to freak out
to freeze
to freshen up
to fret about
to frighten
to fritter
to front for
to frost over
to froth up
to frown
to fumble
to fume
to fuss

G

to gag
to gallivant
to gallop

to gamble

to gang up

to gape at

to gasp

to gather

to gawk

to gaze

to gear up

to generalize

to get a grip

to get a rise out of

to get in one's face

to get off your chest

to get on one's case

to get on the good side

to get out of a jam

to get out of a mess

to giggle

to give

to give out

to give up

to glance

to glare

to glaze over

to gleam

to glean

to glide

to glisten

to gloat

to glory

to gloss over

to glow

to glut

to gnaw

to go against

to go all out

to go along

to go overboard

to go into orbit

to go on and on

to go out of bounds

to go out on a limb

to go to pieces

to goad

to gobble

to goof around

to goof off

to goose

to gore

to gorge

to gossip

to grab

to grant

to grapple

to grasp

to grate

to greet

to grin

to grind

to gripe

to groan

to groom

to groove

to grope

to gross out

to ground

to grovel

to grow

to growl

to grub

to grumble

to grunt

to guard

to guess

to guide

to gulp

to gum up

to gun down

to gush

to gussy up

to guzzle down

to gyp out

H

to hack

to haggle

to hail

to ham up

to hammer

to hand out

to hand over

to hang around

to hang back

to hang in

to hang on

to hanker

to harbor

to harden

to hark

to hark back

to harness

to harp

to hash over

to hassle

to haul

to haul off

to have it out

to head off

to head out

to heal

to heap

to hear

to hear out

to heat up

to heave

to hedge

to help

to hem in

to herd

to hesitate

to hew down

to hide

to high pressure

to hike up

to hinder

to hint

to hire

to hiss

to hit

to hit below the belt
to hit on
to hit up
to hitch
to hoard
to hobnob
to hold against
to hold back
to hold down
to hold in
to hold off
to hold out
to hold up
to holler
to honor
to hoodwink
to hook
to hook up
to hoot
to hop
to hope
to horse around
to hound
to hover
to howl
to huddle
to hum
to hunch over
to hunger
to hunker
to hunt
to hurl
to hurry
to hurt
to hush
to hustle
to hype
to hypothesize

I

to ice up
to identify
to idle about

to idle away
to idolize
to illuminate
to illustrate
to imagine
to imbue
to immerse
to impale
to impart
to impel
to impinge
to implant
to implicate
to impose
to impress
to inch
to incite
to incline
to include
to indicate
to indoctrinate
to induce
to indulge
to infatuate
to infect
to infer
to infest
to infiltrate
to inflict
to inform
to infringe
to infuse
to ingratiate
to inhibit
to initiate
to inject
to inoculate
to inquire
to insinuate
to insist
to inspire
to instigate
to instill

to instruct
to insure
to interfere
to intermingle
to interpret
to intertwine
to intervene
to interview
to intimidate
to intoxicate
to intrigue
to introduce
to intrude
to inundate
to invest
to invite
to invoke
to iron out
to isolate
to issue
to itch

J

to jab
to jabber
to jack around
to jack up
to jam
to jangle
to jazz up
to jeer
to jerk
to jest
to jet
to jibe
to jimmy
to jockey
to join
to joke
to jolt
to jostle
to jot
to judge

to juggle
to juice up
to jumble
to jump
to justify
to jut out

K
to keel over
to keep
to keep after
to keep down
to keep from
to keep up
to kick
to kick around
to kick aside
to kid around
to kill
to kink up
to kiss
to kiss off
to klutz around
to knock
to know about
to knuckle
to kowtow

L
to label
to labor
to lace into
to lag behind
to lam into
to lament
to languish
to lap
to lapse
to lash
to last
to latch
to lather
to laugh

to laugh off
to launch
to lavish
to lay
to leach
to lead
to leak
to lean
to leap
to learn
to lease
to leave
to lecture
to leer
to legislate
to lend
to lengthen
to level
to levy
to liberate
to lick
to lie
to lift
to light
to lighten
to liken
to limber up
to limit
to line up
to linger
to link
to liquor up
to list
to listen
to litter
to liven up
to load
to loaf
to loan
to lob
to lobby
to loiter
to loll

to long for
to look
to look away
to look down
to look forward
to look over
to loom
to loosen
to lop off
to lope along
to lord over
to lose
to lounge
to luck into
to lull
to lumber along
to lump together
to lunge
to lurch
to lure
to lurk
to lust
to luxuriate

M
to maintain
to make a pass
to manage
to maneuver
to map out
to mar
to march
to mark
to marvel
to mash
to masquerade
to measure
to meddle
to mediate
to mellow out
to melt
to mention
to mess

to mess around
to mess up
to mill around
to mingle
to minister
to mislead
to moan
to model
to monkey around
to mooch
to moon over
to mope
to motion
to mourn
to mouth off
to move
to mow down
to muddle along
to muddy up
to muffle up
to mull over
to murmur
to muscle
to muse
to muss up
to muster up
to mutiny
to mutter

N

to nag
to nail
to name
to narrow down
to needle
to neglect
to negotiate
to nest
to nestle
to nibble
to nick
to nip
to nod

to nod off
to nominate
to note
to notify
to nudge
to number
to nurse
to nuzzle

O

to object
to obliterate
to obsess
to offend
to offer
to ogle
to ooze
to oppose
to opt
to ordain
to order
to orient
to oscillate
to oust
to overflow

P

to pace
to pack
to pad
to paint
to pal around
to palm off
to pan
to pander
to panic
to parade
to pardon
to pass over
to pat
to patch up
to pattern
to pave

to pay back
to peck
to peek
to peel back
to peep
to peer
to peg
to pelt
to pen up
to penalize
to penetrate
to pep up
to pepper
to perch
to percolate
to perform
to perk up
to permit
to persecute
to persevere
to persist
to persuade
to pester
to peter out
to petition
to pick
to pick apart
to piddle
to pile on
to pilfer
to pin
to pinch
to pine after
to pine away
to pivot
to plague
to plaster
to play
to play along
to play around
to play down
to play into
to play up

to plead
to please
to pledge
to plod
to plonk
to plot
to plow
to pluck
to plug
to plummet
to plump down
to plunge
to plunk
to point
to poison
to poke
to polarize
to polish
to ponder
to pontificate
to poop out
to pop out
to pop up
to pore over
to portion out
to portray
to pose
to possess
to postpone
to posture
to pounce
to pound
to pout
to practice
to praise
to prance
to prattle
to pray
to preach
to preface
to prefer
to prejudice
to prepare

to prescribe
to press
to pressure
to presume
to pretend
to primp
to probe
to proceed
to prod
to prohibit
to promise
to promote
to prop up
to prostrate
to protect
to provoke
to prowl
to prune
to pry
to puff up
to pull
to pull together
to pump
to punch
to punish
to purge
to purr
to purse up
to push
to push ahead
to pussyfoot
to put off
to put on
to put over
to put up
to putt
to putter
to puzzle

Q

to quail
to quake
to quarrel

to question
to quibble
to quiver
to quiz

R

to race
to rack
to radiate
to rag on
to rage
to rail
to railroad
to rain down
to raise
to rally
to ram
to ramble
to rank
to rant
to rap
to rasp
to rate
to rattle
to reach
to rear back
to reason
to reassure
to rebel
to rebuke
to recall
to recede
to reckon
to reclaim
to recognize
to recoil
to recommend
to reconcile
to recover
to reel back
to reflect
to refrain
to refresh

to reign
to rejoice
to relax
to relinquish
to remark
to remember
to remind
to reminisce
to repel
to report
to reprimand
to reproach
to request
to resign
to rest
to retaliate
to retire
to retreat
to retrieve
to revel
to revenge
to revolt
to reward
to rid of
to rifle
to rip
to ripen
to rise
to rival
to roam
to roar
to rob
to rock
to rocket
to roll
to romp
to root for
to route around
to rub
to ruffle
to rule
to ruminate
to rummage

to rumple
to run
to rush
to rustle

S

to sack
to sacrifice
to safeguard
to sag
to sail
to salute
to salvage
to satiate
to satisfy
to saturate
to saunter
to save
to savor
to scale down
to scamper
to scare
to scatter
to scoff
to scold
to scoop
to scoot
to score
to scour
to scout
to scowl
to scramble
to scrape
to scratch
to scream
to screw around
to scrounge
to scrub
to scuff
to scuffle
to scurry
to scuttle
to seal

to seam
to search
to secure
to seduce
to seethe
to seize
to serve
to settle down
to shake
to shear
to shelter
to shield
to shift
to shine
to shiver
to shock
to shoo
to shoot
to shore up
to shoulder
to shout
to shove
to shovel
to show off
to shower
to shriek
to shrink
to shrivel
to shroud
to shrug
to shudder
to shuffle
to shush
to simmer
to sink
to skid
to skim
to skip
to skirmish
to slack
to slam
to slant
to slap

to slash
to slice
to slick
to slide
to sling
to slink
to slip
to slither
to slobber
to slosh
to slouch
to slug
to slump
to slur
to smack
to smash
to smear
to smile
to smirk
to smooth
to smuggle
to snap
to snarl
to snatch
to snazz
to sneak
to sneer
to sniff
to snitch
to snoop
to snort
to snuggle
to sob
to sparkle
to spatter
to spaz
to speculate
to spew
to spice
to spin
to spiral
to spit
to splash

to splatter
to splinter
to splurge
to sponge
to spoon
to sport
to spout
to sprawl
to spray
to spread
to sprout
to spruce
to spurt
to sputter
to spy
to squabble
to squander
to squash
to squeak
to squeeze
to squint
to squirm
to squirt
to stab
to stack
to stalk
to stall
to stammer
to stamp
to stampede
to stand
to star
to stare
to stash
to steal
to steam
to stimulate
to sting
to stir
to stoop
to store
to storm
to stow

to strain
to strand
to strap
to stray
to stream
to stretch
to stride
to strike
to strip
to strive
to stroll
to struggle
to strum
to strut
to stumble
to submit
to sulk
to summon
to surge
to surrender
to swab
to swallow
to swarm
to sway
to swear
to swear off
to sweep
to sweeten
to swell
to swerve
to swindle
to swirl
to swish
to switch
to swoon
to swoop
to sympathize

T

to tag
to taint
to take
to talk back

to tally
to tamp
to tamper
to tangle
to tinker
to tap
to target
to tattle
to taunt
to tax
to tear
to tease
to tempt
to tend
to terrify
to test
to testify
to theorize
to thrash
to threaten
to thrill
to throw
to thrust
to thud
to thumb
to tick
to tickle
to tidy up
to tighten
to tilt
to tinker
to tip
to toddle
to topple
to torment
to torture
to toss
to tote
to toughen
to tout
to tower
to trace
to trade

to train
to tramp
to trample
to transfer
to trap
to tremble
to trick
to trifle
to triumph
to trot
to tumble
to tussle
to tweak
to twiddle
to twinkle
to twist

U

to unify
to unite
to unleash
to urge

V

to value
to vanish
to vary
to veer
to venture
to verify
to vie
to visit
to visualize
to volunteer

W

to wade
to waffle
to wage
to wager
to wait
to wallow
to waltz

to wander
to wangle
to ward off
to warn
to wash
to wave
to weave
to weep
to whack
to whine
to whip
to whirl
to whisk
to whisper
to wiggle
to wimp
to win
to wink
to wish
to withdraw
to wither
to wobble
to wonder
to worry
to wrangle
to wrap
to wrench
to wrestle
to wriggle
to wrinkle
to writhe

Y

to yammer
to yank
to yak
to yearn
to yell
to yield

Z

to zip
to zing
to zig-zag

Bibliography

Ackerman, Diane. 1991. *A Natural History of the Senses*. New York: Vintage.

Albee, Edward. 1962. *Who's Afraid of Virginia Woolf?* New York: Penguin.

Alderson, Richard. 1979. *Complete Handbook of Voice Training*. New York: Parker.

Anderson, Virgil A. 1977. *Training the Speaking Voice*. 3rd ed. London: Oxford University Press.

Barry, Lynda. 1993. *The Good Times Are Killing Me*. New York: Samuel French.

Beckett, Samuel. 1958. *Endgame and Act Without Words*. New York: Grove Press.

Best, David. 1974. *Expression in Movement and the Arts*. London: Lepus.

Burder, Melissa, and Lee Michael Cohn, Madeleine Olnek, Nathaniel Pollack, Robert Previto, and Scott Zigler. 1986. *A Practical Handbook for the Actor*. New York: Vintage.

Celichowska, Renata. 2000. *The Erick Hawkins Modern Dance Technique*. Hightstown, NJ: Princeton Book.

Charlton, W. 1970. *Aesthetics: An Introduction*. London: Hutchinson.

Chekhov, Michael. 1953. *To the Actor*, New York: Harper and Row.

Cohen, Bonnie Bainbridge. 1993. *Sensing, Feeling, and Action*. Northampton, MA: Contact Editions.

Csikszentmihalyi, Mealy. 1990. *Flow: The Psychology of Optimal Experience*. New York: Harper and Row.

Damasio, Antonio. 1999. *The Feeling of What Happens: Body and Emotion in the Making of Consciousness*. New York: Harcourt Brace.

Dewey, John. 1980. *Art as Experience*. New York: Perigee.

Douglas, Stanley. 1950. *Your Voice: Applied Science of Vocal Art*. New York: Pitman.

Evans, Blakemore G., with J. J. M. Tobin, eds. 1997. *The Riverside Shakespeare*. Boston: Houghton Mifflin.

Fry, D. B. 1979. *The Physics of Speech*. London: Cambridge University Press.

Galati, Frank. 1990. *John Steinbeck's The Grapes of Wrath*. New York: Fireside Theatre.

Goleman, Daniel. 1995. *Emotional Intelligence*. New York. Bantam.

Grotowski, Jerzy. 1968. *Towards a Poor Theatre*. New York: Simon & Schuster.

Harrop, John. 1992. *Acting*. London: Routledge.

Hawkins, Erick. 1992. *The Body Is a Clear Place*. Pennington, NJ: Princeton Book.

Henley, Beth. 1986. *Crimes of the Heart*. New York: Viking.

Hornby, Richard. 1992. *The End of Acting*. New York: Applause.

Inge, William. 1990. *Four Plays*. New York: Grove Weidenfeld.

Kaufman, G. S., and Moss Hart. 1939. *The Man Who Came to Dinner*. New York: Random House.

Kaufman, Moises and the members of Tectonic Theatre Project. 2001. *The Laramie Project*. New York: Vintage.

Keleman, Stanley. 1979. *Somatic Reality*. Berkeley, CA: Center Press.

Kepner, James I. 1993. *Body Process*. San Francisco: Jossey-Bass.

Krasner, David. *Acting Reconsidered*. Unpublished.

Kushner, Tony. 1993. *Angels in America*. New York: Theatre Communications Group.

Laban, Rudolph Von, and F. C. Lawrence. 1974. *Effort: Economy in Body Movement*. Boston: Boston Plays.

Langer, Susanne K. 1942. *Philosophy in a New Key*. 3rd ed. Cambridge, MA: Harvard University Press.

———. 1953. *Feeling and Form*. New York: Charles Scribner's Sons.

———. 1957. *Problems in Art*. New York: Charles Scribner's Sons.

———. 1964. *Philosophical Sketches*. New York: Mentor.

Linklater, Kristin. 1976. *Freeing the Natural Voice*. New York: Drama Book.

Lawrence, Jerome, and Robert E. Lee. 1979. *Inherit the Wind*. New York: Bantam.

Mamet, David. 1978. *Sexual Perversity in Chicago*. New York: Grove Press.

Marrone, Robert. 1990. *Body of Knowledge: An Introduction to Body/Mind Psychology*. New York: State University of New York Press.

McKinney, James C. 1994. *The Diagnosis and Correction of Vocal Faults*. Nashville, TN: Genevox Music Group.

Metcalfe, Steve. 1983. *Strange Snow*. New York: Samuel French.

Middendorf, Ilse. 1990. *The Perceptible Breath*. Paderborn, Germany: Junfermann-Verlag.

Miller, Arthur. 1976. *Death of a Salesman*. New York: Penguin.

Miller, Richard. 1996. *The Structure of Singing*. Belmont, CA: Wadsworth.

Moore, Sonia. 1960. *The Stanislavski System*. New York: Viking.

Northrop, F. S. C. 1962. *Man, Nature, and God*. New York: Simon and Schuster.

Oida, Yoshi. 1997. *The Invisible Actor*. London: Routledge.

O'Neill, Eugene. 1956. *Long Day's Journey into Night*. New Haven: Yale University Press.

Passons, William R. 1975. *Gestalt Approaches in Counseling*. New York: Holt, Rinehart, and Winston.

Richards, Thomas. 1995. *At Work with Grotowski on Physical Actions*. London: Routledge.

Reichmann, James B. 1985. *Philosophy of the Human Person*. Chicago: Loyola University Press.

Rosenberg, Jack Lee, with Majorie L. Rand, and Diane Asay. 1985. *Body, Self, and Soul: Sustaining Integration*. Atlanta, GA: Humantics, Ltd.

Ryle, Gilbert. 1949. *The Concept of Mind*. London: Hutchinson and Company.

Schechner, Richard. 1973. *Environmental Theatre*. New York: Hawthorn.

Shaw, George Bernard. 1970. *The Bodley Head Bernard Shaw: Collected Plays with Their Prefaces*. London: Bodley Head.

Shanley, John Patrick. 2005. *Doubt: A Parable*. New York: Theater Communications Group.

Shepard, Sam. 1985. *Fool for Love*. VHS. Directed by Robert Altmano. Santa Monica, CA: MGM Home Entertainment.

Shultz, Jonathan. 2006. *Open-Ended Scene*. Unpublished.

Skinner, Edith. 1990. *Speech with Distinction*. Revised by Timothy Monic and Lilene Mansell. New York: Applause.

Smith, Edward W. L. 1985. *The Body in Psychotherapy*. Jefferson, NC: McFarland.

Stanislavski, Constantin. 1936. *An Actor Prepares*. New York: Routledge.

———. 1961. *Creating a Role*. New York: Theater Arts.

Sweigard, Lulu E. 1974. *Human Movement Potential*. New York: Harper and Row.

Todd, Mabel E. 1937. *The Thinking Body*. Princeton, NJ: Princeton Book.

Tormey, Alan. 1971. *The Concept of Expression: A Study in Philosophical Psychology and Aesthetics*. Princeton, NJ: Princeton University Press.

Turner, J. Clifford. 1950. *Voice and Speech in the Theater*. London: Pitman House.

Wilder, Thorton. 1957. *Three Plays: Our Town, The Skin of Our Teeth, and The Matchmaker*. New York: Harper.

Williams, Tennessee. 1955. *Cat on a Hot Tin Roof*. New York: Penguin.

———. 1975. *A Streetcar Named Desire*. New York: Penguin Putman.

Zarelli, Philip B. 1995. *Acting (Re)Considered: Theories and Practices*. London: Routledge.

Index

size, modifications or
changes in, 40–43
and sound in
improvising in the
first function, 147–48
in standing exercise
creation, 131
thigh socket in (*see*
Thigh socket)
Movement center
exercise, 78–79

Nasal cavity, as
resonator, 60–62
Nasal resonator, 61–62
No Exit, 191
Northrop, F. S. C., 8,
191–92

Objective feelings, 193
Objectives and
expressive actions,
differences between,
4–5
Oida, Yoshi, 197
O'Neill, Eugene, 179
Open tone, 63, 64
Oral cavity, as resonator,
60–62
Orators, 167
Orientation
in body movement,
45
in breath managment,
55–56
in expressive
continuum, 25
in expressive cycle,
19–20, 22
in improvising in the
first function, 142,
144–45
in sound production,
70
Othello, 180
Our Town, 178

Panting
in breathing center
awareness, 50–51

in breathing center
exercise, 79–80
Parallel leg swings
exercise, 95–97
Part-by-part approach
to training, 30
Partial bridge exercise,
86–87
Passing sensations, 2–3
Pelvic tilt exercise,
84–85
Pelvis, in movement
progression, 37–39
Peripheral breathing,
50–51
Pharynx, as resonator,
60–62
Phrasing
in improvising in the
first function, 139–41
in lying and breathing
exercises, 83
in tuning and
sounding exercises,
106
Physical intelligence,
intuition as type of,
12
Physical phrasing,
exploring, 152
Physical properties,
exploring, 156–57
Physical properties of
expressive action,
17–29
application, 28–29
expressive continuum
(*see* Expressive
continuum)
major properties (*see*
Expressive cycle)
minor, 23–25, 29
Physical tasks, exercise
for performing,
184–85
Pinter, Harold, 135
Pitch, in tuning and
sounding exercises,
106
Playing the text, 166–67

Poetry, as expressing
feelings, 15–16
*Practical Handbook for
the Actor, A,* 195
Practice and theory,
separation of, xvi
Prespeech, 147
Progression
in breath management
49–51
in body movement
37–40
in expressive
continuum, 25
in expressive cycle, 20–
21, 22
in improvising in the
first function, 142–43
in sound production,
66–70
Prompts, in improvising
in the first function,
138–39
Psychological feelings,
193

Radical, empirical
immediacy in art,
191–92
Range, in standing
exercise creation, 132
Rasa, 196–97
Real feelings, 193–96
Rehearsals, expressive
actions in, 5–7
Relaxation
in body movement, 45
in breathing, 56–57
Release
in body movement,
44–45
in breath management,
53–55
in sound production,
59–60
Resolution phase of
expressive cycle, 18–
19
Resonance, 60–62
Resonators, 60–61